Samuel Brackett Wing

The Soldier's Story

A Personal Narrative of the Life, Army Experiences and Marvelous...

Samuel Brackett Wing

The Soldier's Story
A Personal Narrative of the Life, Army Experiences and Marvelous...

ISBN/EAN: 9783337115944

Printed in Europe, USA, Canada, Australia, Japan

Cover: Foto ©ninafisch / pixelio.de

More available books at **www.hansebooks.com**

The Soldier's Story.

A Personal Narrative

OF THE

Life, Army Experiences

AND

Marvelous Sufferings Since the War

OF

SAMUEL B. WING.

PHILLIPS:
Phonograph Steam Book and Job Print.
1898.

S. B. WING AT THE PRESENT TIME.

Introductory.

This soldier's story has been of great interest to me.

To the veteran of the war it will call up his own experiences and make him, in a measure, live again those stirring days. To the wives and mothers, who stayed at home while the loved ones went afield, it will bring back a flood of pathetic longings and yearnings that will once again make the heart tender, and now make it devoutly thankful for the good providences that have, even at so large a cost, given us a re-united and prosperous country. And to the readers of a younger generation this little book, in its simple, quaint, soldier's style, will lift the veil of one of the world's greatest dramas and aid in giving an intelligent and sympathetic appreciation of the awful ordeals which were passed through for the Nation's perpetuity and welfare.

History has not been written until the life and experiences of the *people* have been described. Nor will the narrative of the great war of the rebellion have been penned until, to the account of famous battles and to the praise of renowned generalship, have been added the simpler, yet no less truthful tales of the private soldier, who left his farm or his shop and marched to the camp and the field to do and to suffer all that a patriot's duty might impose upon him.

May the wish of the author be fulfilled, and the mission of these pages be accomplished in "doing good."

ALFRED WILLIAMS ANTHONY,

Lewiston, Maine.

Preface.

Truth is often stranger than fiction. Facts that seem impossible are hard for belief, even when proved. One man may live through experiences that a hundred others could not endure. My story is an example of this kind. I frequently call it the story of the man who was killed, but did not die. If, before the war, I had been told what wounds I should receive, I should have expected nothing short of an army burial, and yet I remain after thirty-three years a living monument that all things are possible with God.

Kind reader, this little book is given to you that it may increase your faith in the power of God. To benefit, as well as interest my readers, is my highest aim. If this narrative of my life will help some young person to avoid the pitfalls set for the unwary, if it shall afford comfort to some afflicted one of maturer years, if it shall add to the faith of some doubter, the author will be amply repaid, even though the book brings to him neither fame nor fortune.

I have tried to give the plain, unvarnished facts, without embellishment or exaggeration. I have endeavored to be concise and correct. Ponder well before you turn from this story thinking some of its statements cannot be true. For the reliability of the author and the truthfulness of his narrative I can refer you, among those still living, who were witnesses of my sufferings, to Mrs. N. S. Whitman, Lewiston, Me.; Mrs. V. A. Barden, Reed's Mill, Me.; Mr. Elias Keene, North Turner, Me.; Mr. M. Campbell, North Turner Bridge, Me.; Mr. A. W. Davenport, Phillips, Me., and Mr. H. S. Wing, Kingfield, Me.

To the kind friends who have nursed me, helped me, and sympathized with me in my varied experiences I extend my hearty thanks; and also to all those who have aided me by counsel and encouragement in the preparation of these pages.

But to you, dear reader, I now submit this little book, hoping that, as out of the untold sacrifices and sufferings of many lives have come to us the blessings of a great and good Republic, blessings too great for any man to compute, so by the narration of the humble, but trying experiences of one who sought ever to do his duty and be "faithful even unto death," there may come to you an increase of faith and courage as you struggle over the hard places of life, and that peace, prosperity and happiness may be your reward.

That the story will interest, instruct and help upbuild you in every good word and work is the great desire of

THE AUTHOR, S. B. WING,

Phillips, Maine.

CHAPTER .

EARLY DAYS.

At what age a child may first receive patriotic impressions is not for me to say. Among my earliest recollections are the stories of the revolutionary war told by my father and grandfather which gave my young mind martial and patriotic feelings deep and lasting.

My grandfather Wing was born in the town of Wayne, Me., and when a mere lad went into the revolutionary war. In one battle he received a severe wound in the leg, and, while lying on the ground anxiously peeping over a stone-wall in order to see how the battle was going, he was struck again by a bullet, this time in the head, so severely as to knock him senseless, though not killing him.

When grandfather at last recovered his senses, he found that our side had been driven back and that he had fallen into the hands of the British. So loyal was he to the cause of his own people and so bitterly did he hate their enemies that he would not permit the British nurses or doctors to dress his wounds and care for him. In consequence of the out-of-doors exposure and this neglect of care, the leg grew so bad that at length it was necessary to amputate it; and my grandfather, who himself became a doctor, ever after had to wear a wooden leg. But he had rather be loyal and patriotic with one leg than to have two and in any measure surrender himself to his country's foes.

That wooden leg used to be the occasion of capers and pranks sometimes among the children. Of course grandfather's step could always be known by the thumping sound made by that wooden leg, and grandmother could always tell when he was coming home from visits on his patients. If he ever happened to be kept from home longer than grandmother expected, she worried about him a great deal. Then my father would take a stick of wood, and coming into the barn and the shed, hobble around with that in imitation of the wooden leg.

As soon as grandmother saw who it really was, she would say, "You little rascal, I'll pay you for that." But father's judgment was better than his courage and he would run away, preferring to have her charge the bill than to settle it with him then.

Grandmother was a very strong woman. It was told of her that she once carried a sack of four bushels of salt up stairs.

Grandmother had five children. My father was the oldest son. He was born in 1792. He received a liberal education in his youth and became a physician like his father. He served as a soldier in the war of 1812. He married Miss Mary B. Norcross of Fayette, and began his practice in Solon. Afterward he moved to Phillips, near Madrid; and then moved into what is now known as the Wing or Prescott district, about four miles and a half from Phillips village. There I was born on March 8th, 1832.

I have always had the influences of a Christian home. As far back as I can remember mother was a firm Christian, and a member of the Free Baptist church. Father, although not a professor of religion, was yet upright and honorable, a man of stern integrity and unflinching moral principles. His word was law, and yet he was not severe with us children. I never in my life received corporal punishment from either father or mother.

The school district in which we lived was almost a model one, until I was nearly fifteen. There was no one in the district who used profane language, and I do not call to mind that I ever in my life used an oath. To say I was an average boy in our neighborhood is equivalent to saying that I was a good boy, for all were clean-mouthed, wholesome lads.

EARLY DAYS.

I speak of this to show my young friends that the surroundings and companions of youth have a lasting influence upon us. If we sow wild oats when we are young, we cannot reap wheat when we are old. The garden that is kept free from noxious weeds in the spring will not be a hard garden to clear from weeds in the summer and in the fall will yield a good harvest. These good habits of my early years gave me a good constitution, without which I never could have endured what I have since been called upon to pass through.

My father's family consisted of five boys and three girls. We had a large farm and had plenty of healthful out-of-door exercise. I always did my share of the work, both about the buildings and in the field.

Although possessing a large share of caution, yet, by my older brothers, I was always called the unlucky child. Perhaps you will agree with them when you have finished my story. The first thing I called my own was a calf of which I took great care and was justly proud. It grew well and was very promising until it was a year old. That spring it got into a bog-hole and died, and I was left without a calf.

When I was quite a boy there was a wonderful Fourth of July celebration at the village. A company of infantry was formed, one of cavalry and a mock tribe of Indians. I belonged to the infantry. During some manœuvres on a cross road just outside of the village, the cavalry horses became frightened and rushed in among us who were on foot. I with some others was thrown over a stick of timber that lay beside the road and my gun was discharged, wounding my hand in four places, tearing the flesh almost from the thumb, injuring the palm and the middle and little fingers. One of my companions had his vest blown to pieces, but he was not seriously injured himself.

This was my first accident, and a forerunner of what I was to see, hear and feel in later days. I was unlucky not because

I was reckless or careless, as it seems to me, nor because of the drinking habit, a habit I never formed. Although we had but little knowledge of the destructive power of alcohol in our quiet neighborhood, yet I never liked the accursed stuff. Temperance was not a common theme of lecture or sermon in our hearing. Even some ministers in my day took a little wine or whiskey, "for their stomach's sake," I suppose.

Sometimes I was sent to procure liquor, but even then I was ashamed of my errand and used to go away off through the fields and unfrequented roads so as not to be seen. But as it was used so freely and was called so good as medicine, I would be persuaded to take a little for the purpose of breaking up a cold or curing some other ailment. At times, too, when treated, I would take a little for fear of being called odd, but instead of forming an appetite for it by such use I liked it less and less.

One of our neighbors said to me one day:

"Liquor is good in its place, if people would take just enough."

"How much is just enough?" I asked.

He did not answer, and just then the truth dawned upon me.

"Just enough is none at all," I said.

"You are right," he replied; "You are just right."

This was my first temperance declaration, and to my surprise it obtained the approval which I have ever since desired for the same sentiments, an approval which my own judgment has repeatedly affirmed as I have seen the disastrous consequences of trying to take "just enough."

In the fall when I was nineteen or twenty years old, my father and I, with some neighbors, were lumbering in the woods about ten miles from home. We used to go in on Mondays and come out on Saturdays. On the way we passed a place where liquor was kept for sale and used to stop for drinks. I made up my mind that that was bad business, and by myself resolved to have nothing to do with it. The next time we came out, I thought to go right by the place, but my companions told me that it was my turn to stand treat and that I couldn't shirk it. Fearing that they would think me penurious, I went in and ordered the treat. When all had taken a glass, they wanted me to drink also, but I refused. Then someone said that I should not pay if I did not drink, and there was some warm discussion. Whether or not, I finally paid for the drinks, I do not remember, but I know that I did not drink myself at that time, nor have I from that day to this, nor have I since then offered to treat others.

From that day, total abstinence has been my motto. That principle has carried me through many hard places. Without it I should not live to tell this story. I have been a close observer of men and things all through my life, and, as I draw near its close, I am more and more impressed with the necessity of the prohibition, "Touch not, taste not, handle not."

To men, young and old, I say beware, beware; let the accursed thing alone; it may ruin you, body and soul; let it alone.

"Many a trouble and many a woe
I've been saved, because I answered no;
Many a sin, and many a crime
I have missed by a no, at the right time.

"Will you take a drink?" the merchant said:
I only had to shake my head.
A shake of the head at the right time
Will keep you, my boy, from many a crime.

"A little no, or a little shake
For God, and the home, and the mother's sake,
Will keep you from many a trouble and woe.
Boys; Remember to say *no*, NO, NO."

CHAPTER II.
CONVERSION.

Now I come to one of the happiest parts of my life.

It was the winter of 1852 and 53. I had been lumbering, as I have already mentioned, and came home in January or February. On my way home I met a man who said,

"You ought to be at home, for they are having a revival."

"A revival?" I said, "It is just my luck to have my porridge dish wrong side up when it rains porridge. I wish I were there."

I said this in a jocular vein, but yet really felt that it was more serious than jocular.

Although a lover of fun, yet I never felt at home with vulgar or profane persons, and it was far from me to make fun, or ridicule sacred things, or to speak lightly of religious persons as a side thrust at religion. From my earliest recollections I always attended meetings and sabbath school. At this time now referred to I did not, however, have the chance to attend the meetings, and I returned to the woods.

But soon after I again came out home, this time for the purpose of repairing the mill, and now I had the precious privilege of attending the meetings. Many of my schoolmates had found peace and joy, and others were fervently seeking for the pearl of great price.

The under-shepherd was Rev. A. H. Morrell, now long since gone to his reward after years of faithful service, many of them spent among the colored people of the South, at Harper's Ferry, West Virginia. If consistency is a jewel, then he was one, a shepherd in deed and in truth. While to those that know him my words will seem exceedingly weak, yet I cannot

CONVERSION.

pass without speaking of a very few of the many good qualities which he so richly possessed. His life was a noble one for imitation. I tell of it that it may be a benefit to us and to all around. But, alas! how few attain to that high standard of precept and example that he daily manifested.

First, I would say, he was an honest man. Surely all ministers should be, yet some, though with right intentions fail in some things for want of caution and judgment. He, however, had strong and clear perceptions of what was right and wrong, and heartily did he carry them out in his life to the very letter. Not nearly right, but just right seemed to be his motto. While you believed in his doctrine, you could not help believing in him. I have heard lectures that were good, but have had no faith in the lecturer, and that spoiled the lecture for me. He made all his promises with caution and with earnestness fulfilled them. While he did not seem to be in a hurry, yet he was always busy and accomplished a large amount of work. He so let his light shine that others saw his good works and were led to glorify their Father in heaven. To let our light shine without flickering or going out, is good and grand, and merits the approbation of all.

He was very sympathetic. In forming his acquaintance you would soon feel his sincere regard for you. In giving you counsel he drew you gently yet steadily toward righteousness and peace.

He was a peacemaker of the first quality, but on Bible principles. To all, high or low, rich or poor, he was impartial in the highest degree. He was ever the same genial man, every day alike, with warm sympathy for all and malice toward none. Homely figures illustrate his merits: he was not like the cow that gives a good mess of milk and then kicks it over. He was like gold tried in the fire. He often said that if people's hearts were all right, their heads would not disagree enough to do any great harm; surely "out of the heart are the issues of life."

He was faithful to the cause of the down-trodden slave at a time when it was very unpopular to be outspoken in their behalf. How often our ears were greeted with what some fastidious and foolish folks call "a minister's dabbling in politics." But what, pray, are ministers for if not to let their light shine even in the darkest places? Or, how will they be guiltless, if the sword come and they warn not the people?

It is high time for us now to beware lest a greater evil than slavery come upon us. The enemy of all righteousness is not dead, but is steadily and stealthily creeping on to Washington; yes, is already there, tightening its coils around us year by year. "Righteousness exalteth a nation, but sin is a curse to any people."

TO THE MEMORY OF REV. A. H. MORRELL.

Tune, "I'm Going Home." Key of G.

His heart so kind was blessings all,
O may this grace on others fall;
The work the Lord by him has done,
May through our lives and actions run.

CHORUS.

I'll meet you there, I'll meet you there,
I'll meet you there where all is fair,
Where all is fair, where all is fair,
I'll meet you there where all is fair.

His prayers and tears so strong appealed,
I'm glad my heart to them did yield;
Since God, my King, was there revealed,
Praise, prayer and faith have been my shield.

CHORUS.

If we lose heaven, we all have lost,
Then we shall know what sin has cost;
If we gain heaven, there's nothing more:
God holds for us all things in store.

CONVERSION.

Chorus.

O what is it to save a soul,
And while eternal ages roll
To be with Christ! The harps will ring;
With heavenly rapture the angels sing.

Chorus.

How many souls will bless the Lord;
Through him they did receive the word,
And did believe and were baptized,
And now will meet him in the skies.

Chorus.

He used to sing of peace and love,
To waft our souls to heaven above:
Then we gained strength to do our part;
Hope, love and joy did fill the heart.

Chorus.

O while I live be this my prayer,
That I may meet and see him there,
And all those glories with him share,
That mortal tongue cannot declare.

Chorus.   S. B. W.

After attending a few of the meetings held by Mr. Morrell, I was deeply interested. Indeed I had been interested before, but delaying to act in keeping with my interest had hardened my heart. While others were feeling deeply, I had no feeling whatever, but looked on unmoved and seemed to myself like a statue, cold and hard. I was willing enough to act, but if I acted it would be without any feeling in the matter whatever. That I didn't like. When at length I rose for prayers in the meetings, it was a great effort because of my perplexities about not having feeling, and I seemed to gain nothing. I thought that if I only had feelings like others, I would make a public confession of Christ; but to confess without that feeling seemed to me to be hypocritical.

There I made a great mistake, for I did not know then, as I do now, that the Lord never intended that one person should wait for an experience like another, but each should be true to his own duties and let his feelings take care of themselves. But I waited. Others about me sought and found peace. Still I waited, and remained the same. But the Lord knows how to bring us out of darkness. He taught me that I had one thing to do and only one thing, and that if I did that everything else would be all right. That one thing was to obey, and then I should receive.

One night after the meetings had continued for quite a while, three or four of us went home together. We all thought it would be the proper thing for us to read the Bible before going to bed. My companions asked me to read, and I was quite willing to do so. Then we were sure that some one ought to offer prayer. But no one was willing. I had no particular objection, excepting that it seemed to be presumption for me, without any more feeling, to take upon myself this sacred privilege. After considerable hesitation, however, I consented.

How much that prayer lacked! Had it thankfulness or praise? No. Had it feeling or emotion? No. Had it earnest pleading or supplication? No. It lacked all these qualities. It seemed to me to lack all the true elements of prayer; and yet that prayer availed with God, for it was really a promise on my part to obey God whether I felt like it or not, to do what he wanted me to do without regard to my feelings in the matter, and to be faithful to my own convictions of duty, whether I was like anybody else or not. That was the first right step I had taken. "Obedience is better than sacrifice." God accepted the promise I then made and the surrender of my will then and there, and I had peace.

S. B. WING—TAKEN WHILE IN THE ARMY.

CONVERSION.

> I felt my heart consent
> God should reign, God should reign;
> I felt my heart consent, God should reign,
> I felt my heart consent,
> But I knew not what it mean.,
> And a sweet calmness went
> Through my soul.

Before retiring for the night we sang:

> "Did Christ o'er sinners weep,
> And shall our cheeks be dry?
> Let floods of penitential grief
> Burst forth from every eye."

I had sung sacred music from my earliest childhood, but never had it made melody in my heart as now. Those words had a meaning new to me and they brought a softening and a calmness of heart such as I never felt before. This experience was so different from any others I had ever had that I hardly dared to acknowledge it. Truly all things were becoming new to me, for things I once hated I now loved. I had done the one thing needful; I had surrendered myself to God and had begun to obey.

As soon as I had an opportunity I made public confession of him. God took me up out of a horrible pit of miry clay and put a new song in my mouth. God had shown me that to yield my will to him was all that was necessary for me and that he would do the rest. That was the great lesson of my life. Happiness and peace came to me then and have ever since been my portion, and in obeying and trusting God I have found strength for all my trials and sufferings through all my life. It is His power that has carried me through what I have yet to relate.

CHAPTER III.

MARRIAGE.

A number of years passed. My family still called me the unlucky one, for I kept on having some kind of accident happen to me off and on. Once I came near having my legs crushed between two logs, but managed to escape with a severe sprain of the ankle.

But now I come to the love story of my life. In this I was not a bit unlucky. I cannot tell all the best parts of that story, for such things cannot be told, and I never had a fondness for love stories, they seemed to me either too silly or too sacred to tell right out in public to all the world.

But pure love is the best attribute that has been given to mortals, and there is nothing grander, nobler, or more beautiful, nothing that can elevate us and bring us nearer to the image of God than love, pure and undefiled, for God is love himself. Like gold, love is good money in any part of the world; and like gold, it has been counterfeited, until it is almost impossible to tell the good from the bad. As with gold, too, love has been used to gild the most heinous characters, and the less the real worth, the greater the polish oftentimes given to the gilding, so that many of the young without experience in life take the gilt in preference to the solid gold. But, alas! how very soon the baser metal shows, and then the tender hopes are crushed to the ground.

It was in the fall of '55. We were having lyceums at the Reed schoolhouse, some three miles from my home. From this little red schoolhouse went forth many eminent men to do good work in the world. It is possible that the color of red paint has something to do with the education of young children,

MARRIAGE.

as they are fond of bright colors and are stimulated by whatever pleases the fancy or arouses their admiration. But more likely the success of the red schoolhouse of those days was due in greatest degree to the spelling schools and lyceums held in them, that gave the young such a wide field of thought in the subjects discussed, and trained them so closely to observe and to remember both words and facts for future use.

This I have learned, that it is not the schoolhouse that makes a successful school, nor the books and maps alone, but the training and discipline to independence and manliness. It is best to avail ourselves of every opportunity for improvement. Then success is sure to follow.

On this special evening which I have in mind, I had been appointed to give a declamation, but I had not received word of my appointment until it was too late to prepare myself for it, and so I asked to be excused and gave my reason. Brother N. C. Brackett, who is now well-known as the president of Storer College, Harper's Ferry, West Virginia, was then the presiding officer, and he seemed somewhat unwilling to accept my excuse. No doubt he has had boys many a time begging off from work with similar excuses, when there was really no good reason for excusing them. He did not say much, but yet it was enough to touch me quite a little. I didn't say anything, however, but took a back seat and tried to swallow my chagrin.

The question for the evening was:

RESOLVED, that the western states give greater inducements to young men than the eastern states.

I think this must have been after the famous advice of Horace Greeley, "Go west, young man, go west."

I remember I was on the negative side, and as I was little excited and exasperated already by the experience of the evening, I didn't take much care with what I was to say. I loaded pretty heavy without much reference to sense, if only I could make a noise. I didn't go out to the front, but stayed where I was, by that back seat.

In the course of my argument I made a good many strong assertions without any positive knowledge on my own part. I talked about the western mud and the mud houses out there and pictured the circumstances just as bad as I could. Of course I was talking for effect, but it didn't dawn on me then as it has since, that every time I said a thing I didn't know I was really lying. I was. But as the others didn't know much more about the subject than I did, no one could gainsay my assertions, and so they passed with many as facts.

Another thing that evening of which I am now ashamed I will relate, for it was under just such circumstances as these that I met her who afterwards became my wife.

I always prided myself on good behavior both in public and in private. But this evening I was sitting on the back seat, as I have said, a seat which ran clear across the schoolhouse, and it was full. We all whispered a good deal and I suppose disturbed the proceedings. I happened to have a pocket full of spruce gum, and taking pieces of that out I passed them to the next one to me with the hint, "Go west, young man," and the gum started; and pretty soon every one on that back seat was "yanking gum", as we called it. If I had seen Mr. Brackett doing that I should have been ashamed of him. But that evening I felt like humoring myself; and I did.

After the lyceum was over, on my way out, I met a young girl of perhaps fifteen summers, a fair blonde and to my eye most attractive. The aisle was crowded and no one seemed in a hurry. The pretty girl and I fell into conversation which seemed to interest us both. As we neared the door, she innocently inquired, if I was going her way. Without asking which way that was I answered yes, for under the circumstances I didn't feel like saying no; and guessing that perhaps they went across lots, I said nothing about my horse which was hitched out among the trees, waiting for me. It was just a young colt, and had been taken out of the thills while he was standing.

So I went along with the young lady, chatting most pleasantly. She had two sisters with her, one younger and one older. But another young man, perhaps having lost his way, was walking with the older sister.

We soon left the main road and took a path across lots, up a steep hill and over fences, where the ground was rough and uneven and it was necessary to help the girls along pretty often.

But we reached the grandfather's house at length, where the young ladies lived, and were invited in. The old folks had retired and the fire in the stone fireplace had been covered up for the night, but we were comfortable and had plenty to talk about, so much so that the older sister and the young man with her wondered at our talking so constantly.

But the fact is, for forty years after we never lacked subjects for pleasant and helpful conversation.

Well, when that young man and I at length took our departure, we came along the main road together a little distance, and then he turned to the right and I to the left. When I reached the school house, how surprised I was to find colt and wagon both gone: After a little reflection, however, I reached the conclusion that some of the boys to play a joke on me had taken the horse and left me to get home afoot, and I thought I should find the horse either at home or on the road. I was quite sure there was no one who desired to injure me maliciously, for I stood on good footing with all the young people of the neighborhood. Probably they had seen me start off with the young lady and had thought it too good a chance to lose for some innocent fun.

But there I was with a long walk ahead of me. With a reflective mind I started for home. What was my surprise before I had gone many rods to hear my colt whinnying to me, as much as to say, "Don't leave me; here I am." I presume he had heard my heavy footsteps in the still night air.

Horse music may be coarse, but I was in just the right frame of mind at that time to enjoy just such music. It was sweet to my ears, and exactly adapted to my circumstances. Adaptation makes every thing fit in its season, and I appreciated it then.

I turned in the direction of the sound, with a much lighter heart and a much quicker step, and a few rods back from the road, in an entirely new place to me, I found my colt and wagon. The horse was securely tied, and to judge of his actions was as glad to see me as I was to see him. Horses I know are not so hypocritical as men, and do not put on feelings which they do not feel.

The boys who had played this trick on me had hauled the wagon over a tumbled down fence, and, as wagons were heavy in those days, it was not an easy task for me to draw it back again. The colt was so young and so nervous from long standing that I did not dare to hitch him into the wagon and try to drive him out over the fence. So I kept on pulling and managed to work the wagon along little by little until it was clear out. To have gone to the neighbors and call for help would have been just the chance the boys wanted for poking fun at me, and I was fortunate to escape their hands in this way.

I got home finally all right, but I never knew who played the trick on me, nor did the perpetrators ever have the satisfaction of finding out how I recovered my horse and wagon, for if they saw me the next day, they heard me whistling and singing as ever. I seldom got so irritated that I could not sing or whistle without outward sign of disturbance. In this way I have escaped a great deal of teasing in which young people are very apt to indulge with each other; for if a man does not seem to mind and goes right along about his business, they will let him alone and try some one else who is less fortunate and shows his vexation.

Self-control and calmness under provocation will save you from a great deal of trouble and annoyance. A good share of our misfortunes come from looking at things wrongly. I remember a man with whom I had been acquainted from boyhood came to me once very much excited because some people had been lying about him as he said, and he denounced them severely. I heard him through quietly and then remarked that I did not consider myself too good to be lied about. To say that he was thunderstruck at my seeming indifference may be putting it pretty strongly; but he soon quieted down, lost all his excitement and got over his worry. That was the best way.

If we consider Him who bore such contradictions of sinners, who when he was reviled, reviled not again, what magnanimity is shown in all his life! Oh! that by beholding we might be changed into His image.

Although "a lie can run forty miles, while truth is pulling on his boots," yet the lie does not run in a straight direction and can be headed off. So tired and worn out will the lie become that truth can kill it with one blow.

Another instance of the necessity of keeping calm and of being truthful I must give you. On one occasion when there was a gathering at one of the neighbors, I was so busy that my wife went on in advance of me and I followed later. The people had heard of something that I had said and done and as my wife knew nothing about it and could give no explanation, they had decided my case before I arrived, had pronounced me guilty and had severely condemned me, and had me all ready for the halter.

As soon as I came in, they asked me if I had really said and done so-and-so.

I answered, "Yes, I did, exactly that."

And then I went on and told them the circumstances and how it came about, giving a full explanation of the case. When I had finished, the one who had censured me the most severely said,

"You did just right. I would have done the same."

After my side of the story had been heard they all justified me in the course pursued. And then again I saw, as I have often had occasion to observe, that it is better to admit the whole truth at the outset than to try to keep back a part, and it is also necessary to avoid forming hasty judgments; we should be careful not to form a too strong opinion until both sides have been heard. You must know that there is not much truth in half the lies that are told.

Well, I must resume my love story.

My regard for Miss Mary A. Lufkin, with whom I went home from the little red schoolhouse that evening, kept on increasing. We had opportunities, and made a great many others, for meeting. At length we were united in marriage, August 2, 1857, in Phillips, Maine, by Rev. A. H. Morrell.

Losing her father when quite young, my wife had been away from home during most of her girlhood, but this did not break her attachment for home.

> "Home, home, sweet home,—
> Be it ever so humble,
> There's no place like home."

It is one thing to like a home, and another to make a home and adorn it. My wife possessed both qualities.

It was just before our marriage that the serenade craze broke out in those parts of the country. Some objected to this kind of treatment, and at times quite a feud would be kindled between neighbors. The services were carried on without much ceremony and without a "by your leave." I rather objected to this kind of a celebration, but I was not to be overlooked. I had made up my mind, however, that I would not open my house to the crowd, if they came.

Well, one night they did come, from north, east, south and west, with all kinds of instruments of noise, such as trumpets, tin pans, cow-bells, and the like ; in fact every thing that would swell the racket and tend to make the night hideous. There was din enough to awaken the heathen gods.

After they had played some of their best pieces, they gave me an invitation to come out and meet my friends. But as I did not train in that company I did not appear to roll-call. They seemed quite patient at first at my non-appearance, but soon began to be more and more in earnest, and redoubled the fury of their racket. But at this crisis, fortunately for my wife and me, there came up a very heavy thunder shower, such as was never more welcome in the time of severest drought. Our serenaders couldn't stand the drenching long and, receiving no invitation to shelter, concluded to return home.

How glad we were that it was over, and we supposed it over.

We often go beyond ourselves, and when we undertake a thing and find it harder than we expected, then we feel just so much the more determined to push it through, at whatever cost. While this is a most noble quality when exerted in a righteous cause, it is most despicable when used in any wrong or mean way. To be brave and determined in a good cause is commended by God and man ; but to be set and obstinate and persistent in mischief is to be pig-headed and nothing else. In the one direction a man becomes a hero : but in the other he becomes a brute.

My serenaders seemed to me to be of this second kind. For the next two nights they let me alone and I began to think that that was an end of the whole matter ; but fate and the boys did not so decree. The third night they came again and with reinforcement and more determined than ever. They commenced about where they left off before. After they had demonstrated their ability to make a noise for a good long time, they demanded that I should come forth and show the bride or they would come in and see her. But, as on the other night, I made no reply, knowing full well that I could do nothing parleying with them, and I was pretty confident that they would not try to break in, for there were many in their own company unwilling to go so far, and besides it would take a good deal of courage to break into a man's house when he was in the way, and it was dark.

They then held a consultation of war and decided that I had got to come out by hook or by crook, and they would try crook first. So they next let down the bars and began shouting that the cows were in the corn.

Well, that ruse came out about as Gran Gould's pig did. Some one asked him how much his pig weighed. He replied that it did not weigh as much as he expected and he did not think it would either.

I did not come out at that call as they expected, and they didn't think I would either. But they succeeded in getting my younger brother out, and he told them that I slept in a bedroom on the back side of the house. Then they declared that they would take me out of the window. And five or six of them set about doing it. But it was a job that required more courage than they then had.

Just as they arrived at the back of the house, some one sung out,

"Look out! He's after you!"

And another such stampede has seldom been witnessed this side of Bull Run. Out back of the house was a sag in the ground filled with rain from the recent showers and with drainings from the barn, making a mixture that no gentleman would want to put his foot in. This in their blind rush in the darkness they did not notice, and a number of them went splashing through the mire, about knee deep, wetting their feet and legs, much to the delight of one who had taken no part in the serenade.

This wetting dampened their courage as well as their legs, and soon retreating footsteps were heard and a comic song, which one of them struck up as they moved away, wishing us

"A good night's rest without a wink of sleep."
And a good breakfast without a blank think to eat,"

and assuring us that the next time he called he would kiss the bride. (A promise that was never fulfilled to my knowledge.)

Some may object to the way I treated these serenaders, as though I was unwilling to associate with them and enter into their innocent fun. But that is not it. They were what folks would call "good-hearted boys," but they didn't act in a real good-hearted way. I object to calling those good-hearted who, though social, obliging, industrious and liberal, yet persist in profanity, vulgarity, rowdyism, foolish jesting and other things of a similar nature.

No word in the English language has been more abused than that word good, for the devil and his co-adjutors make great use of it. They speak of good rum, good whiskey, good brandy. It would be just as well to say good woe, good misery, good destruction. Many say, "I had a good time on a drunken spree." I think they had better qualify it and say, as one did in my hearing, "I had a hellish good time."

I have no fellowship for such times and shall ask to be excused, let people think what they will.

I learned afterwards that another company came up near our house, but did not think it best to ask me to open the house, even to a mixed company, and so they went away.

There is a great difference between who and what we are. The careless, disorderly and rowdyish do not fare the same as the considerate, courteous and kind, any more than sinners receive the same as the saints. "And we know that all things work together for good to those that love God," while they do not work in any such way for the ungodly.

  Be kind and be gentle, be fervent, devout,
  Have faith and righteousness to drive away doubt!
  Oh! take the right road and ne'er turn about,
  And then you will know just where you'll come out.

CHAPTER IV.
LIFE IN THE AROOSTOOK.

After marriage we lived one year in Madrid, above Phillips and then in 1860 we moved to Maysville, now Presque Isle, in the Aroostook County.

It was, I think, in 1861 that diphtheria commenced its ravages in Aroostook and other places in Maine. In this I had quite an experience. Whole families were dying off with it in our vicinity. We had two children then, and being much alarmed for their safety we did not go about very much and so hoped to avoid the contagion.

But one Sabbath morning my wife said that her throat felt badly. I replied that mine felt badly too. She said she would go up stairs and lie down.

It was in September. We had a fire in the stove. I put my feet in the oven and, leaning back in my chair, fell asleep. When I awoke, I had been sweating profusely. In two or three days my wife had grown worse, so that she came very near strangling to death, while I was able to be around the house. But, strange to say, she recovered from it and the children did not even come down with it.

As others needed help I would sit up with them.

At that time the doctors did not know much about the disease. One would give one thing, another another thing. One would keep his patients full of whiskey, another would use lobelia as a specific. But three and four were dying in a family.

Once when I was sitting up with two little girls in one family, the doctor came. One girl was so low that he could do nothing for her, and he gave her nothing. To the other he gave as much whiskey as she could take and this one was the one to die first. I made up my mind then and there that whiskey was not good for diphtheria.

After this I was quite free in expressing my opinion about how the disease should be treated. One young man out of whose family four children had already died after having been treated in the whiskey-way, said to me that if he had the disease he wanted me to have care of him and treat him.

Well, soon after this he came down sick, but his friends sent for a doctor first. Then, twenty-four hours later, I was sent for. The first twenty-four hours is the most important time for breaking the hold of the disease upon the system and I didn't want to take hold of the case under this disadvantage. But the young man was very urgent and so I began to treat him, for sure death seemed in store for him if he was treated as the others had been.

The next twenty-four hours gave me hope, and then he gained steadily until in four days' time he was able to sit up a good deal. Being at home that afternoon, I went down to see him just at night and found him worse. It came to me in a moment that the doctor had been there.

I said to him, "You are worse?"

"Yes," he replied.

"Has the doctor been here?"

"Yes."

"And you have taken his prescription?"

"Yes."

"Then I will have nothing more to do with you. You were getting along well, weren't you?"

"Very well," he answered; "and I want you to tend me."

I said, "I cannot, for the doctor's methods are right opposite to mine."

He begged me hard, and promised to follow my way exclusively.

Just then his father came in, and made some pretty hard talk to me about my meddling with a doctor's patient and upsetting the doctor's treatment, and said that if they employed a physician they were going to follow the physician's directions.

After the father went out, I told the boy that I could not do any more for him. But he pleaded with me as one would for his life.

I said, "You know how I was treating you and you were getting along first rate, but I cannot go against your father's wishes." And so I left him.

But the next day the father came to my house and said that his boy wanted me to go down. I went down, and found him better than I had feared. Fortunately he had taken but one dose of the whiskey. I took care of him in my way and the young man got well.

I treated four in one family who had been given up by the lobelia doctor. One breathed so hard that you could hear him quite a distance. But they all recovered.

One of my patients, after getting well enough to come to the table, wanted pork and potatoes to eat. I objected, but he ate them, thinking they would not hurt him. Soon he was taken with stoppage and died. Any one convalescing must be very careful about what he eats and about taking cold.

I attended quite a number of cases and, when called in season, had remarkable success. In most instances they did not keep their beds more than one or two days and got along so well that some said it was not true diphtheria, but I have seen too many cases to be mistaken.

I must add my own experience in the winter of 1880, in January, I believe. We had six children then, the youngest two and a half years old and the next ten years old. This ten-years-old one was the one to come down first. I was sick in bed at the time, with my army wound, about which I am to tell you later.

LIFE IN THE AROOSTOOK.

The little girl said her throat felt badly. My wife looked in and said there were diphtheria spots there. She knew them, for she had seen enough of them. My wife thought best to put a pork rind on her throat. But the child grew worse and we sent for a doctor. He changed the throat pack to hot soap suds. But still the child kept growing worse.

On the third night her breathing was so hard that I said to my wife, "I am afraid we are going to lose her."

She replied, "I know it, but what can we do."

"Call Herbert," I answered.

Herbert was then twelve years old. I told him to go to the store, three quarters of a mile distant, and get a bottle of opodeldoc and a bottle of Johnson's Anodyne Liniment.

These were procured, and we commenced bathing the child's throat with the opodeldoc. In less than one hour she began to breathe more easily. We used the opodeldoc until the outside of the throat was too sore for its application and then we put on the anodyne liniment, and her permanent recovery was under way.

Our little boy of two and a half years' age was the next to come down with it. This is a bad age to treat for it is hard to make them do as you want them to, and they cannot often gargle at so young an age. He had quite a severe attack, but we succeeded in our care of him and had him up and about the room in four or five days.

The next one was our oldest boy, who had been having a hoarse cold for several days. He went to the village and on coming back, a very cold evening, went straight to bed without warming himself, as the kitchen fire was out. About four o'clock in the morning we heard him call. His mother got him down stairs. He said he had been calling to us about all night. And what a looking sight he was! His face was all purple and his throat had bad looking patches. But we began to treat him right away. He was old enough to obey instructions and commenced to gain immediately and in four days we had him well enough to want to go out, but this was not permitted for he would surely have had a relapse, if he had gone.

Kind reader, with no other motive but your good, I will give you my method of treatment, and I hope it will be the means of saving the lives of many dear children. Do not think it is too simple, or that it is too much bother to undertake it, and do not delay a moment when you have good cause to think a child has the diphtheria, for the first thing to be done cannot be done too soon. Hoping that you will be thorough with the treatment and that you will have the same results that I have had I prayerfully submit it to you.

1st. Give a teaspoonful of sweet spirits of nitre, if the patient is fifteen years of age, or in like proportion according to age.

2nd. Give a thorough sweat. My method is, if in winter, to have the temperature of the room up to about 70, then to heat green wood very hot, wrap it up in cloths and put it in the bed. This green wood will give out moisture as well as heat. Let the patient drink as much water as wanted, either hot or cold. Heat soapstones and wrap in damp cloths. Be sure to make them sweat freely for at least one hour and then let them cool off very slowly. Indeed if they sweat for from four to six hours, all the better.

3rd. One-half hour after commencing the sweat give a good dose of pills, or castor oil. This is very essential. Repeat the dose, if not effective and thorough.

4th. Have the throat gargled. It does not matter so much what is used, provided the throat is kept moist. A little salt and pepper (not strong) in water is good. Chlorate of potash is, also, good. Gargle every few minutes. Do not let the throat become dry. If the patient is too young to gargle, then let him hold the liquid in his mouth a moment and swallow a little of it. Do not let the patient sleep more than a half hour without gargling. This will seem hard at first, but must be persisted in. Many will say "Don't disturb them; let them sleep all they can." But this is fatal.

5th. As for diet:— For the first, second and third days do not say anything to the patient about food. No one will starve in that length of time. If they call for food, then give a little of thin gruel, or milk, a very little at a time. How many times I have heard people say, "You must eat something to keep up your strength." But, dear reader, until the disease is fully broken up, you are feeding the disease. They do not need food of any kind at the first.

6th. Never bundle or pack the throat. Bathe it rather with some good liniment. Johnson's Anodyne Liniment, opodeldoc, or alcohol are good for this purpose. Rub lightly, if not too sore. In stubborn cases this should be used every hour.

7th. Use common sense. I mean by this, dear reader, do not mix this treatment with some other for every one will have some advice to give; and do no get worried. The patient must necessarily breathe hard for the first few nights, but if the breathing is deep, not short and quick, there is no cause for alarm. Keep an even temperature at about 70 degrees by day and not below 60 at night. Do not use the fan, unless on some special occasion.

Dear reader, if this terrible scourge should ever visit your home, I hope you will have the same success with this treatment that I have had and may preserve an unbroken family. I believe that nine out of every ten can be saved by this method of treatment.

In the winter of 1862 we lost our little boy, Silas M. Wing, a very loving and interesting child. Death was caused by his being scalded. He was two years old.

> A promising child to us was given,
> By angels carried back to heaven:

> Rest, dearest, rest;
> And by your side some sweet day,
> We with the angel host will say,
> God knoweth best.

The Aroostook was very different from our old home, but it was a fine country, with many advantages as well as disadvantages. We found the land excellent for cultivation, rich and easily cleared and producing large crops of wheat and oats. Sometimes we raised one hundred bushels of oats to the acre. It was just the country for the potato too. We raised large crops of these.

We were surprised to find so much lime in the soil, and in the water, so that water boiled in kettles would make the kettles white inside. It was strange, too, to find the land so free from stones. No great piles of stones disfigured our Aroostook farm, and told of backaches in getting them together. There were not even stone enough to build a cellar and the cellars in our vicinity were "stoned" with cedar logs. Cedar grew plentifully.

Different classes of people were around us, but all were neighborly and industrious. We liked the Aroostook land and people and were glad we had made our home there.

There were some disadvantages, however. We were very far from market, at that time farther than now, for we had no direct line of railroad to connect us with the other parts of the state. The summer seasons were very short, and the winters long. Still they were not so windy as with us in Franklin County, and we were not so troubled with drifting snows. The first year I was in the Aroostook, I think we broke out the roads only once. There was a snow storm in September of that year, about the 20th, as I remember it, when six inches of snow fell and stayed on the ground for a few days, lodging the grain very badly; but that was something the oldest settlers had never seen before.

CHAPTER V.

GOING TO THE WAR.

In the summer of '63 Government did a very foolish thing in a call for soldiers by draft and then after that offering a very large bounty for volunteers. You will readily see how this worked. It would cause many to go under very unfavorable circumstances. The rich, if drafted, could hire substitutes, but the poor must go, regardless of how they left their few belongings and their loved ones behind.

My circumstances were these:—I had moved to the Aroostook away from all relatives.—I had just started on a farm and had good prospects of success, yet I was poor. I had a young wife and two small children, with no one near in whose care they and the farm could be left, and there were many about ready to take every advantage of the absent ones.

I was drafted. What was I to do? I went. Crops, almost ready to harvest, were nearly lost by neglect. Leaving things to the mercy of others found but little mercy. For example, I had a pair of fine cattle, on which a man had a claim of a little more than half what they were worth. I left on such short notice that I did not have time to sell the cattle, and so I left them with a neighbor to sell and pay the claim. This would leave me something over. But as soon as I had gone the man who had the claim on them came and took them and left me nothing.

Then I had a fine cow which I left with a neighbor to sell. He kept her until the first of winter, fed her on my potatoes and then charged me for keeping her nearly all she brought. Certainly a cow like that ought to have paid for her keeping.

Other things went in the same way. When I say that I lost

nearly all that I had, there is no exaggeration in the statement. Not being able to go back, I never was in a condition to get any redress.

So before you censure, or stigmatize the drafted man, just put yourself in the same situation, and you can judge rightly how much he sacrificed and what it cost him to serve his country. The drafted men were just as brave as any, far more honorable than the bounty jumpers. The stigma of coward thrown at them is unjust. They sacrificed more than many others and got less. Even after the war when Government undertook to equalize the bounties, the drafted men were thrown out. I leave it with you to say whether this was just.

My wife was too young to leave in charge of the farm, and we thought it best for her to go to her folks and stay with them while I was away. So in 1863 we came back to the old homestead in Phillips, she to stay and I to move on to the front.

I spent two weeks with father, mother, brothers, sisters, friends and neighbors, and after this I was going to Dixie's land, perhaps never to return. The soldier had to think of the uncertainty of life as few other men did. It behoved him to be ready at any moment to give an account up yonder. I wonder how any man could go into battle without having first made his peace with God. Indeed I wonder how any man can do anything or go anywhere without first reconciling his soul to God. Life is so uncertain; it ends so quickly.

I will not try to depict the parting scene. Those who have had a like experience know too well the feeling of leaving the loved ones with so little prospect of a return, yet trusting that all will come out well in their case at least.

I set forth to help save my country. I stopped first a few days on Mackey's Island in Portland Harbor. Here I found one of my old schoolmates, Joseph Plummer, and others of my acquaintance.

From there we went to an island in Boston Harbor. There

we drilled some, though not enough to hurt any one. There we met a great fighter from Aroostook. No one dared to put the gloves on with him. Some remarked that he could whip a regiment of rebs. But when we really got down south and out on the field and were expecting a battle, he shot his thumb off. He told the doctor that it was an accident, but comrade Plummer saw him do it and said that it was done on purpose. He was sent back to the hospital, and we never saw him again. So much for a man who could whip a regiment!

It is one thing to whip a regiment when you are talking about it, and a very different thing to really do it. He looked at bullets differently from what he did at boxing gloves.

We took a steamer from Boston to Alexandria, setting sail just at night. The wind had been blowing for a few days and it was pretty rough. Many were seasick, but I escaped this. That was a dismal, sorry night, that first night out on the way down south and so many sick. But the next day it was better, and so the boys began to be more cheerful.

The second night had fun in it. Some of the boys went to the top of the stairs, where there were some hams, and taking one threw it down stairs. It made a terrible stir and racket. Then in a moment all was still. The officers came around to see if they could find the one guilty of throwing the ham; but no one knew anything about it.

Soldiers would have their fun, and it is well that they would. Many a gloomy hour and many a sad spirit were lightened up by the pranks played by the soldiers, and courage was often quickened by the laughter caused by the fun and mischief. Fun that has no unkindness in it need never be objected to.

The day before we went up Chesapeake Bay I saw a man punished. What his fault was I do not know. But the punishment was just horrible. He was gagged by having a stick tied into his mouth, his hands were tied behind him, and he was strung up in the rigging so that he could barely touch his toes and most of his weight was on his hands. He seemed to be in terrible agony, and when taken down was hardly able to speak or move and seemed almost dead. Such barbarity of punishment I thought too heathenish to be tolerated for a moment.

It was a fine October morning when we sailed up the Chesapeake Bay. Never having been on the ocean before this voyage and having been out three days, the bay seemed like a new world to me. Its waters were smooth, the steamer steady and the scenery beautiful. We could see the home of Washington in the distance. But though this scenery and these surroundings were so delightful, yet they must all pass and trials and hardships be encountered.

"Slowly sailing, slowly sailing, hushed the music, mute the mirth,
U. S. soldiers standing reverent on some broad altar's hearth."

* * * * * * * *

"Silently before Mount Vernon, silently our boat moves on,
Hushed the iron heart's deep panting past the tomb of Washington;
Truest, worthiest act of worship that degenerate earth now knows,
Inmost-soul here recognizing all the mighty debt she owes.
O, my country! art thou paling—losing all the young day's glow?
Canst thou lose thy first love's glory and thy hero's worth still know?
Patriot hearts, no doubt, still haunt you, threatening thoughts
    come crowding on,
Sail with me up broad Potomac, past the tomb of Washington:
Feel the impress of his greatness stamped upon the Nation's heart,
See each manly brow uncovered, stern lips in awe apart;
Fear not while this reverence lingers with its warm, clear, hallowing
    light;
This must fade from brow and bosom, ere can come our country's
    night."

Arriving at Alexandria, we marched up through the city and saw signs on some of the buildings, marked in great black letters, "SLAVES FOR SALE."

In the streets we were halted. The citizens came out of their houses with pies, cookies and other goodies, which were a rare treat for us who had been kept for a long time back principally on soups, called by some of the boys, "slops." And to say that many of the men who had money indulged their sharpened appetite.

Other of the citizens, standing in doorways and other places, plainly told by their sullen looks that they had no welcome for us or friendly feelings.

Then we marched up to the barracks, an old slave-pen, where, no doubt, hundreds of slaves had awaited their destiny. We had hopes of again meeting our loved ones at home, but for the slaves there had been no hope; and of what treatment he was to have a slave could have but little conception. The horrors of slavery came over me as never before when I tried to sleep for the first time in an old slave-pen, by the very walls that had kept a poor black man from his freedom and had heard his awful agony of sorrow.

During the night some of the men were taken sick, and the doctor was sent for. He came and, smelling their breath and looking them over, turned and went out with this remark,

"They will be all right in the morning."

Then we mistrusted what was up. The boys had secured some bottles of the devil's fire-water, and had been imbibing too freely. That is what had made them "sick." They had been willing to forge another link in the chain which when once around a man holds him in a more galling slavery than that our prison-pen had known.

The next morning we took train and went to Manassas Junction, and there we joined the Army of the Potomac.

Why are all these men here? A well-known cause actuated the Government. But the men had different motives, among which during my army experiences I found the following:—

Some had come because of a reckless spirit of a hurly-burly, don't-care kind, eager for excitement and thoughtless of consequences. Others because of the bounty promised and expected. Others were there in consequence of their bravery and daring. Others thought only of their country's welfare.

But why was I there? I had been drafted, to be sure, but that was not the only reason of my coming. No; my judgment had been active; I had been thinking and had formulated in my mind good reasons why I should be in the army and why, being there, I should make of myself a good soldier.

I was not there because I thought myself brave, nor because I liked excitement. In fact I should have made a good Quaker, had it not been for reasonings like this:—The rebellion must be put down; if it is not, the consequences upon human welfare and happiness seemed to me awful; and then, if it must be put down, whose duty is it to go and help? Was it not every good citizen's and patriot's? Then, why not mine? Was there any reason for me to be excused? Couldn't every man be excused, if I could be? Then, who would protect the country? It seemed selfish to desire a good government and not be willing to help make it so.

Such thoughts as these justified my presence in camp and made me regard my being there as a matter of patriotic duty and not the mere chance of having been drafted.

The army was under the command of Gen. George B. Meade. I was put in the second corps under Gen. Winfield S. Hancock, in the Third Division under Gen. Burney, in the Third Brigade under Gen. Ward, and in the Third Regiment of the Third Maine Infantry.

I do not consider that there was so much difference in the Maine regiments as some have thought. Some of the regimental officers had a gift of writing home in praise of their regiments, conveying the idea that they were doing the greater part of the work.

The old Third Maine was not detailed for guard duty, but was continually at the front and could be depended upon every time.

But the old soldiers, when they saw the raw recruits, had many misgivings. Some called them a "mess of cowards." We heard it on every hand, until after the first fight. Then we heard something like this,

"How did the recruits stand the fire?"

"Oh! They did not know enough to run."

And then the fellowship between the old and the new soldiers was better established.

While these pages are not designed to portray great battles or to laud great generalship, yet I would like to express my opinion of the merits of some, from my point of view.

In my humble opinion some have received honor and praise which was due to others. For an illustration, we will suppose a man is going to build a house. He selects eight or ten skilled workmen, and secures one for boss, or overseer. When all is completed, you take a friend to view it. He asks,

"Who is your masterworkman?"

You say, "Mr. Grant."

Well, we find pieces of very excellent work in various places throughout the building, and the credit all goes to Mr. Grant. But in making closer inquiry, the friend asks,

"What workman executed this?"

We learn that this was done by Mr. Meade, and we doubt if even the boss could have done so neat a job.

And again we find another very fine piece of workmanship.

"Who did this?"

"Mr. Hancock."

And still another.

"This was done by Mr. Burnside."

And so on.

We deem it fair to give to each one the praise for what he actually did. I believe some of the other generals in their places accomplished just as much as did Gen. Grant in his, and if they had been in his place they would have done as well as he, with the same authority as lieutenant general, not only with the right to command but also with the right to call upon other troops. My object is not to detract from Gen. Grant's praise, —that is too firmly fixed,—but that other generals may receive the honor they so much deserve.

The commander of our corps, Gen. Hancock, is well known in history and is credited with being a hard pusher, for he pushed the enemy hard and dealt solid blows. Many a day, while I was in the army, our corps lost as many men as all the others. Gen. Burney, successor of Gen. Kearney, commander of our division, was known as the bravest of the brave.

I remember hearing a song while in the army which the soldiers very much enjoyed.

"McLellan made a movement,
 He made it rather slow,
In the old Virginia low land, low land, low;
 The rebel general found it out
 And pitched into his rear,
 But he'd better have seen the devil
 For he found old Kearney here;
In the old Virginia low land, low land, low."

CHAPTER VI.
CAMP LIFE.

We remained at Manassas Junction nearly a week engaged in drilling and learning the details of camp life. Then, a pleasant day, we were ordered out on a march.

Along in the afternoon we heard cannonading. We halted in a field where once in a while a stray bullet whistled by; and where we could see the shells going over our heads to visit the rebels. But we were not called into action.

Just at night we started again and crossed the Rappahannock river. It was about waist deep. One man was killed by a stray bullet while crossing the river.

We camped for the night, wet, hungry and tired. It was a very cold night in November. I was being initiated into army life a little.

The next day was pleasant. It was on this day, while we were getting ready for marching, that our hero (spoken of before) shot off his thumb.

We took up our line of march, and, hearing nothing from the rebs, we halted between Brandy Station and Culpepper, and went into camp. Here we stayed some two or three weeks, until some time in December, when an order came from Washington for us to attack the enemy.

Why had we delayed so long? This brings up the old familiar saying, "Why don't the Army of the Potomac move?" It was only a repetition of Burnside's experience in attacking Fredericksburg, waiting until after the roads had become almost impassible.

The nights were so cold that the men suffered exceedingly.

It seemed foolish to try to drive the rebs out of their stronghold with but few more in number, and also to keep up a supply for the army over such roads, roads that were all mud and water. The poor horses would sink in so that it would seem almost impossible to move on. The blows and curses of the drivers were horrible in the extreme. And the soldiers wading in the water in cold December weather would to the fearful seem like wading to their death.

Be it said in praise of Gen. Meade and other generals that the army was brought back to the old camping ground without any mishaps.

Now we are ready to sing,

"Tenting to-night, tenting to-night,
Tenting on the old camp ground."

For a few weeks now everything common to camp life went on quietly. As my health was good, I employed my spare time, when not on duty, in washing for others, thus earning as much as I received from the government. Hope was good and faith was strong.

What an eager time we used to have of it in looking for a box from home! And when it came, how we then pulled out its contents, as busy and chattering as children over a new toy, and yet at times when a special love-token came to sight, how the eyes would fill up and the voice choke, and then some of the boys would turn away to let you alone for a moment, or one would pat you on the back with a few words of kindness and sympathy. Oh! the soldier, out in the field, had a tender spot under his jacket, and a longing love for home, and a kind regard for his comrades, notwithstanding his fun and his tricks and his pranks.

Then there were the experiences on picket duty, a day or two at a time.

About this time I had an experience, which I shall never forget: I was obliged to witness the execution of a deserter

Friends of humanity, join with me in sympathy for the fate of a young soldier in the prime of life, straight, fine proportioned, weighing about 180 pounds, fine features and complexion, healthy, strong and vigorous. What a sight, to see him marching behind his coffin through the long line of soldiers, then placed on his coffin and deliberately shot!

Some say, it was all right, that he deserved it; but it is more than I ever want to see again, or ever want to carry in my memory long. But we other soldiers could not be excused. We were obliged to look on.

As the young soldier passed us, he looked around, for he belonged to our company. I was not in the army when he deserted and was not acquainted with him, but of course what he had done and all about him had been common talk in the company and I had heard it all.

His name was Hunter. He deserted and joined the rebels. [And a cousin by the same name soon got a short furlough and then left for good.] He was taken prisoner and condemned to this sad fate, but he seemed wholly indifferent to it. The chaplain, who walked beside him, told me that he was perfectly unmoved and unconcerned. Oh! how hard the human heart can become! If he could have said with Paul, "I am now ready to be offered, and the time of my departure is at hand. I have fought a good fight, I have finished my course, I have kept the faith; henceforth there is laid up for me a crown of righteousness, which the Lord, the righteous judge, shall give me at that day."

> "Vain man, thy fond pursuits forbear,
> Repent thine end is nigh;
> Death, at the farthest, can't be far,
> Oh! think before thou die."

On the 14th of January we moved our camp about three miles, and commenced making our tents which, in this place, were built of split logs of fine white oak covered with tent cloth.

Generally four men were convened in a tent, but in our case there were but three. Wheeler, Taylor and myself. Wheeler was older; Taylor was only a boy.

Let us look inside of the tent. In one corner was a fireplace, made of mud and sticks, or rather of sticks covered with mud. This was where we did our cooking, and it helped to give cheer, too, by its warmth and light. A rubber blanket served as door. Bunks were on one side, one above the other A box that came from home constituted our table, chairs, bandbox and cupboard. That box was enough to make a good man happy, coming, as it did, just as we were building our tent.

Can you imagine the joy that a soldier would feel when he saw a box that the dear ones at home had sent him? There would be in it all sorts of things to make him comfortable: boots to replace the army shoes, socks and gloves and shirts and handkerchiefs, and almost every thing that you can think of. And if a soldier had more of one thing than he needed, he could exchange with some one else for another thing that he wanted, or he could sell at a good price and then with his money buy something else.

I was glad that I found in my box no such present as one of he boys did in his. Hidden away in one of the boots that came to him was a flask of whiskey, with which he made merry and got drunk. And when we were ordered out on a march, he was left behind in camp *catching white mice*. And when we returned in four days, they were carrying him out with muffled drum to his grave. So, you see, that man lost his life by this little flask of whiskey.

Oh! that destroyer of mankind, worse than war, pestilence or famine. While we deplore war, we wink at intemperance.

In the march spoken of, we marched all day, then halted for the night and made ourselves quite comfortable for the night as the weather was pleasant.

CAMP LIFE.

The next day was fine. Some cavalry passed by us. We heard firing in the distance. In the afternoon it looked like rain. So we began to prepare for the night by making shelters with rails and our rubber blankets stretched over them. During the night we had a cold storm of rain and sleet.

In the morning, while I was up building the fire, Wheeler, my tentmate, was in the tent yawning and throwing up his hands. Once he hit a fold of the rubber blanket above his head, containing about a pailful of rain and sleet, and brought this down all over him giving him a pretty good drenching. How he jumped and sputtered! And how we laughed! This was rare sport for the soldiers and helped to keep off the blues.

We learned that our marching out this time was to co-operate with the cavalry, who were reconnoitering around Richmond. (This was the time when they were led wrong by a negro, the only instance known during the war.) And when the tired cavalrymen came back, we were to give them a chance to get into camp and stop the rebs, if they followed.

On the fourth day we were back in camp again and resumed the duties of picket, campguard, drilling, inspection, washing, cleaning up, and so on.

One day, while I was on campguard, a comrade, named Mackay, came along and said,

"Wing, if you weren't on guard, I would take hold of you, at side hug, and throw you."

"All right," I replied, "I shall be off very soon, and you can try it."

When I got to my tent and looked up the street, I saw Mackay and one of the sergeants coming. They were not at all backward in stating what they had come for.

Mackay claimed the privilege of having the under hold.

"Very well," said I, "if I can have my right arm."

He was short and my arm came just right for his neck.

We took hold and went at it in earnest. He thought he

could throw me over backwards. I put on what we used to call "the grape vine," and in an instant he was the under man. All the while the sergeant had been calling out to Mackay,

"You throw him or I'll lick you."

As soon as Mackay was up the sergeant started for him to carry out the threat, and Mackay began to run with the sergeant after him.

"Sergeant, hold on," said I, "he did the best he could, and you are not going to lick him for that."

He stopped, and we had a good laugh and parted in good spirits.

Afterwards, when I was in the hospital in Washington, I saw Mackay. He looked well, and I was surprised to see him there, and said to him,

"Mackay, how did you get here?"

He replied in a very low tone so that no one else could hear.

"I will tell *you*, but don't let it get out. I sent home for some poison ivy, and just before the spring campaign rubbed it all over my face. I swelled up fearfully. I told the doctor I was terribly sick and he sent me back here. I have always said that there were not men enough in the army to get me to go into a battle."

"Well, what are you doing back here now?" I inquired.

"O, I have a walk or two to sweep out," he answered.

The next time he was paid off, he wanted to know if I did not wish him to buy me something down in the city. I told him no. When he came back he had lost every cent he had.

Another comrade had a medal on which were inscribed the names of sixteen battles that he had been in. The sergeant told me that he had never been in a single battle. The captain gave orders to the sergeant to place a strict watch over that man and see that he went into the next battle. So when they were marching to battle, the sergeant had the fellow just ahead of him and kept his eye on him. But something took the sergeant's attention for a moment, and when he next looked for his bird, he had flown and was nowhere in sight.

Now, how many such men as these would Gen. Grant need to quell the rebellion? The sergeant himself said to me,

"Talk about courage; there are none here but would do the same thing, if it was not for the shame and disgrace attached to it; I judge all by myself. I do not go into a fight because I like it, and I would not go in, if I was not ashamed to run."

One time, while on campguard, I was kept on duty four hours instead of two, for stopping to get a drink of water. The officer of the day was Capt. Harvey who was killed the sixth day of May. In the battle of the wilderness I was within a few feet of him and saw him when he fell.

Sergeant Emery fell in the same battle. I had had a few words with him because I would not lend money to the boys to gamble with. He called me low, mean, stingy, and all the epithets he could think of. I said nothing for two or three days. Then I thought it was my turn to speak with him.

I told him that I thought he had accused me wrongfully. I had a family at home that needed all my money; and that by keeping a little money by me for times of need I had misused no one. As soon as I could spare any money, I was in the habit of sending it home to my wife and children, while they had larger pay than I and were without responsibilities such as I had. I thought he had no right to call me mean, low or stingy.

He said not a word in reply.

It seemed very strange to me that these two men, the only ones with whom I had had any trouble,—and that very slight,—should be the first to fall in the first and second days fight.

About this time I had occasion to see what the practical value of a good education is. The doctor wanted an assistant to help keep accounts, write letters and so on. I had the chance of the place offered to me. The doctor seemed pleased with me until he examined me in regard to my education and then, finding that he could get a man who had studied much more than I had, he decided to take the other man.

We never can know what might have been.

> "Of all sad words of tongue or pen,
> The saddest are these, it might have been."

If I had had the better education, then I might have been receiving thirty dollars a month as the doctor's assistant instead of but thirteen dollars a month as an ordinary soldier, and might have escaped the perils of the bullets in battle and have been without the wound which I have carried these more than thirty-four years.

How many blessings we may lose by being deficient in this needful qualification! A proper education makes life desirable, it gives enjoyment, it helps show many a pitfall, it lightens our burdens.

While in camp we had brigade meetings every Sunday evening. As I was going down one Sunday, in the early part of April, I saw a young man chopping wood near his tent. I asked him to go to meeting with me. He began to laugh in a very jeering way, and said,

"Do you think I am pious?" and continued to laugh.

I tried to reason with him and convince him that piety would not hurt him but would do him good. But with many oaths and coarse expressions he derided the meetings.

I saw that he would not reason, and so passed on.

But I had a good chance to learn considerable about his history, for he could neither read nor write and used to come to our tent to get my tentmate, Wheeler, to read and write for him. He told me that his mother had written him that she wanted him to send her some money the next time he was paid off, for his father drank so badly that she had been obliged to leave him and she had no way of support.

In a few days we were paid off. And the next day the officers sent word to the soldiers that all who would come and help set out trees around their tents should have all the liquor to drink that they wanted.

This young man with some others went. That night he did not come back to his tent. The next morning when he came back he was without watch or money. The officers promised to try and look it up, but that was the last of it. He never recovered a cent of it, and his mother never received a copper.

It seemed to me at the time like a plot on the part of some of the lower officers to rob some of the poor ignorant soldiers.

Certainly a little piety would not have hurt that poor fellow. Had he but learned a few passages in the Good Book and heeded them, he would have averted all this trouble, and have been a help and comfort to his mother in her trials and afflictions.

Such as these:—"Judgments are prepared for scorners and stripes for the back of fools."

"Wine is a mocker, strong drink is raging, and whosoever is deceived thereby, is not wise."

"Blessed is the man that walketh not in the counsel of the ungodly, nor standeth in the way of sinners, nor sitteth in the seat of the scornful."

"Can a man take fire in his bosom and his clothes not be burned? Can one go up on hot coals, and his feet not be burned?"

"Be not deceived; God is not mocked; whatsoever a man soweth, that shall he also reap."

But this young man did not seem sorry for what he had done, he was only sorry for the consequences, that he had lost his watch and money. He must have had a heart like stone if he did not feel sorry when he learned, as the next letter reported to us, that his mother had been taken to an insane asylum.

But these things did not reform him. On the next pay-day he got so drunk that, wandering out into a field, he could not get back. My tent-mate and myself with some others brought him in and put him into his berth. But a pigpen would be preferable to his tent.

I asked some of his tent-mates to help bring him in, but they said,

"No, let (hic) him stay there (hic.)"

I told them that, as it was just at night and looked like rain, he might die out there.

"Well, let him (hic) die, if he (hic) wants to."

Oh! how a man must despise both body and soul to do such things. At this time nearly one-half of our company was drunk. A fine plight for us to be in, were the enemy to come upon us! We should have been in as much danger of being shot by our own men as by the rebs.

A great many good men tolerated this evil, thinking that it would encourage the soldiers to continue in the army and would also give cheer and strength to others to enlist. But they little thought that they were giving courage and strength to a far greater evil than slavery. For slavery could only chain the body, while intemperance destroys both soul and body. "For no drunkard shall inherit the kindgdom of God."

Dear reader, taste not, touch not, handle not, and you will be saved from one of the greatest curses that now afflicts our land. It is an unequal warfare. Rum beats every time. You will be captured, bound, imprisoned and kept on the meanest of fare, while you boast of liberty and independence. You become the meanest slave that the world has ever known.

A man must hate himself and every one around him, when he realizes what a fool and what a slave he is making of himself, for it amounts to that and nothing else. "Wherefore do ye spend money for that which is not bread, and your labor for that which satisfieth not?"

I have seen considerable intemperance but never knew of its doing any one any good. If it is of advantage to no one and thousands are destroyed by it, then why not let it alone? Why not? WHY NOT? WHY NOT?

> Ah! rumseller, think as you may,
> There comes for you soon a reckoning day,
> Think not to escape that misery and blight,
> For surely for you comes a horrible night.

Now a few words about picket duty. The picket-line extended about three or four miles from the army, and soldiers were sent out in squads, so that about one-third would be on duty at a time. These were placed about one hundred yards apart, and tramped backward and forward on a beat.

Beyond the pickets about two miles was a vidette, so that on the approach of the enemy the vidette would fall back and give information to the picket-line and then to the army.

The picket was to fight a retreat back to the army, and by this time the army would be drawn up in line of battle and ready for action. There were signal stations also in advantageous positions watching the enemy, so that it was next to impossible to be taken by surprise.

One night when I was out on picket and off duty, the sergeant came to me and said,

"You must go and take the place of a man who is afraid to stay on his beat."

The place was near a building and in the building the man had heard noises that scared him. I took his place and watched the night out without hearing anything of any great consequence. In the morning, when we examined this building, we found two old mules quietly munching straw.

There was no great danger that the rebs would fire on our soldiers from that building, for in a trice the whole reserve would have surrounded that house and made escape impossible.

At another time, when I had come off duty and had just got to sleep, some one came, all excited, and awakened me saying, "The rebs are right upon us."

I got up as quickly as I could, caught my gun and started. Others were in advance of me running for a piece of thick woods. Just then a lot of crows started up and made a great flutter flopping away. And that was all they had heard. I called it a very unnecessary crow-scare and we were the scare-crows. We were scared but had no cause to crow about it.

The last of March I wrote home to my brother. He saw my wife and told her that he had had a letter from me, but just to tease her said it was a private letter and would not let her see it.

The next time she wrote to me she said that she thought I might write her a private letter as well as to my brother.

So I went to the sutler's tent and bought a small envelope, and took a slip of paper and wrote on it "April First, 1864; and put it in the small envelope, sealed and marked it private. Then I wrote a letter and put all in a large envelope.

When my wife received it, she took the small envelope and went off by herself to read it. The next letter I received she wanted to know if any one had made a fool of me.

I replied to her, no, for nature had got the start of them.

So you see we took every way we could think of to drive off the blues, which had been the cause of the death of so many soldiers. First they would begin to talk discouragingly and to look very melancholy; and then would be idle a good part of the time about their tents, sad and despondent; and in a short time they would answer to the doctor-call, and soon be admitted to the hospital; and after that it was not long before they would be carried out with muffled drums.

It was best for us, nay, it was absolutely necessary for us to use every means to be cheerful and hopeful and to be busily

CAMP LIFE.

employed, for these would be the means of driving the blues far, far away.

At times the soldiers would get together and sing, and how heartily they would sing! "When this cruel war is over" we sang again and again praying that we might all meet again.

As the spring drew near, we were kept quite busy in drilling, target shooting, picket and other duties, which consumed the most of our time and gave no time for the blues.

April was a cool month for that climate, with considerable wind. We moved our camp about two miles out. This was for the purpose of getting out of winter-quarters and preparing for the field. This was on the 26th of April.

CHAPTER VII.
THE BATTLE FIELD.

The second of May at night we received orders to march. So we thought we must have another dish of the good old army beans. These were baked in the ground, and I believe no better way has ever been found for baking beans, as the moisture of the ground keeps then from drying up. They were cooked until they were cherry-red, and were delicious. The army beans to this day are held in reverence by the old soldiers.

We did not get much sleep that night, for some were taking down their tents and putting their things together, although no orders had been issued to pack up and the pack-up bugle (which was so much disliked by the army boys) had not sounded.

I turned out at two or three o'clock in the morning and went down and got my beans.

Orders to march did not come until between ten and eleven o'clock. Then we marched until about noon, and filed into a field for dinner.

It seemed wasteful to see the overcoats and blankets thrown on the fire. We would not need them and could not carry them longer, and they were burned so that the rebels could not pick them up and use them. Many of them, also, were throw into the mud for miles along the road to make better walking and were trampled out of sight.

We halted quite early that afternoon, and I went on picket at night. The next day we marched nearly all day, and at night I was ordered on picket again. I told the sergeant that

I did not see why I should go on picket two nights in succession. He said he did not know why it was so; he was simply obeying orders. So I went without further hesitation.

We were sent into the woods about two hundred yards. In the morning, when we expected to be called off, we received no orders, but yet heard the army moving.

It was customary to relieve the picket by calling from one man to another down the whole line, and so passing the word along.

We held a consultation and decided to send a man to see why we had had no orders. He followed the picket line until he came out of the woods and then found that it went no farther. The pickets in the field did not know that there were men in the woods and so had not passed the word along to us. And so the army had gone on and left us.

We set out then to join the regiment and get into our company, if we could find it. Soon we fell in with the cavalry and were led a very roundabout way by them.

It was a very hot day and having been broken of my sleep so much on picket duty, I was taken with a very severe headache, and along in the afternoon was unable to keep up with the rest. One of the cavalry men, seeing my condition, dismounted and asked me to ride. I accepted his kindness with a thankful heart.

We went some distance and then were ordered to halt. I dismounted and started to go along afoot. The man who had given me the ride said I looked too sick to march and said he would get me an ambulance and take me to the hospital. I thanked him and said I must try to get to my regiment. As I was already very much rested and it was a little cooler, I could travel with much more ease.

My comrades on picket had gone on ahead and had been out of sight for some time. I had been hearing firing for some time and now it became quite general all along the line.

THE BATTLE FIELD.

After travelling quite a distance I saw the boys who had been on picket with me coming towards me. They had been on the wrong road and were coming back. But just before they got to me or saw me they turned off on a cross road. I hurried and tried to overtake them, but they were going at a very rapid pace and I could not come up with them.

About dark I arrived at a hospital and found that it belonged to my corps. The Third Maine was at the front, as it almost always was. They said it would be dangerous for me to try to find it in the night. But the Fourth Maine was near by; so I stayed with them that night.

I fell in with a man who wished to go to the Third Maine very early, and we started together at about light the next morning.

When we arrived the boys were just building their fires to make coffee. Only a very few had proceeded so far as to get their coffee on to boil, when the order came to fall into line, So there was no coffee for us that morning and no time to eat, save as we could take a bite of hard tack in our hands.

We advanced a little way, and then the battle was fairly upon us. Bullets whistled and cannon roared. We were in the din and the thick of the fight.

Capt. Harvey was killed in the forenoon, and also Lieut. Col. Burt. Some of my comrades fell near me, some dead, others wounded. Comrade Plummer received a slight wound in the hand.

Along in the afternoon the firing for a time quieted down. We were in the woods and could not see what the rebels were planning to do. At our left the line of battle made a curve. At this point the rebels made a furious charge, broke through the line and came in upon us in the rear.

Col. Lakeman, seeing this, called to us.

"Boys, come out of this."

We did not wait for a second or a third invitation. We prided ourselves on being good for a retreat.

The bushes and underbrush were so thick that we had to keep our eyes shut as we forced our way through, or we would have had our eyes put out. Once when I looked up, I had my gun lying right on the colonel's back. (Not much respect for colonels on a retreat!)

Pretty soon the order was, short and sharp,

"Rally, boys, rally; rally round the flag."

The retreat was none too soon, for already some of our number had been taken prisoners.

Perhaps some one may think that we should have stood our ground and fought where we were, but we would not have had time to change our position and draw up with company front toward the rebels before they would have surrounded us, nor could we in that position have used our guns, for our firing would have been lengthwise of our own ranks.

I think in this Battle of the Wilderness the rebels had the advantage. They were near the edge of the woods, and could quickly form their troops, and before we could get any idea of their intentions, they would charge in upon us and break our ranks, taking many prisoners.

After three days I think our generals saw our disadvantage; and Gen. Grant began his flank movement, drawing us out of the Wilderness into Spottsylvania, where we could use our artillery to good advantage. And our artillery was far superior to that of the enemy. In the Wilderness it had been of but very little use. So we began to feel that we were on better footing.

The tenth day we marched out into a field, while the rebels were shelling us pretty lively. Gen. Ward was hit by a piece of shell in the temple. The officers gathered around him for a few minutes. Then he resumed his command, although the blood was still running down his face and on his clothes.

In a short time we were taken behind the breastworks; and along about sundown were ordered out to make a charge over a knoll, or small hill, where the rebels had a heavy battery. This knoll was covered with thick, scrubby pine, so that our ranks were broken in getting through.

The rebel battery was meantime pouring grape and cannister upon us, cutting down our ranks like grass. It seemed as though the air was full of bullets.

We were defeated with heavy loss.

I went back to the hospital with Comrade Bragg, who was wounded in the arm, but I returned in the morning. That day nothing unusual transpired. Along in the afternoon it began to look like rain and we collected boards and rails to make a shelter, but there was to be no rest for the soldier that night.

In the afternoon Gen. Meade received the following dispatch from Gen. Grant, dated at 3 p. m.:

"Move three divisions of the 2nd Corps by the rear of the 5th and 6th, under cover of the night, so as to join the 9th Corps in a vigorous assault on the enemy at 4 o'clock a. m., on the morrow."

We were ordered to get ready without lights or noise. As it commenced to rain, it was exceedingly dark. We were taken across fields and swamps and through the woods, without any roads, often finding ourselves plunged into water nearly knee-deep. If one fell out of his place for a moment, he could not get back into it without calling upon the one with whom he was marching, so intense was the darkness.

And so we marched all night long, hungry, wet and tired. Wouldn't you like to be a soldier?

> Wouldn't you like to be a soldier,
> And hear the bugle call,
> Marching in the dead of night,
> And into a mud-hole fall?

THE BATTLE FIELD. 67

Just before light we were drawn up in line of battle, waiting for the dawning of the morning.

While we are waiting, reader, just look at what was before us. First, there was an abatis, and, lest you may not all know what an abatis is, I will give a brief description.

It is a row of large branches of trees, sharpened and laid with points outward in front of a fortification to obstruct the approach of assailants. The larger ends of the branches are secured to the ground. But this is not an exact description of the one in front of us, for this had been made hurriedly, and was done by felling trees, their tops outward, in front of the breastworks.

As in many places these were scrubby pines, just imagine for a moment a soldier with knapsack, haversack, tenting outfit, rifle, sixty rounds of ammunition, and his canteen, trying to go from the top of a tree through its branches towards the butt. That would be almost an impossibility, and doubly so under the cruel fire of the enemy.

In places where it seemed possible to break a way through, there the soldiers would rush, while those meeting the obstacles spoken of, would turn to the right or the left and so break up the lines and get the companies in confusion. Then at the places where the greatest numbers were with hopes of getting through, there the cannons and rifles of the enemy were directed with deadly effect.

The breast-works were made by first piling up logs in a tier as high as a soldier could conveniently fire over, then this was banked up on the outside with soft dirt so thick that not even a cannon ball of the kind then used would do any harm, and on top of all this would be placed another log leaving just space enough between it and the one beneath for the muzzle of a rifle to be thrust through and fired, without exposing the soldier's head.

So you can readily see what a very great advantage the enemy had behind such breastworks as these.

At last daylight came, as it always does. We marched up through a piece of woods some fifteen or twenty rods. The Irish Brigade was ahead of us, and they did splendid work. They made the assault.

As soon as we heard the firing, we started on the double-quick. When we met the abatis, before described, the whole brigade became mixed up in one mass. But still we rushed on as fast as possible, for an instant of time might save hundreds of lives. Officers could do but little in handling the men, but gave such general orders as they could.

The men seemed eager to do what was best. We followed the breastwork front and rear, surrounded a large number of rebels and captured about two thousand prisoners and took possession of a portion of the breastworks. Then we fell back to a position outside of the breastworks.

Gen. Mott rode along and gave us a high compliment for what we had done. Among our prisoners we had two rebel officers, Maj. Gen. Edward Johnson and Brig., Gen. George H. Stuart. They were ordered to dismount, and were put under a negro guard and were sent to headquarters. Their looks showed that it was specially humiliating to be put under a negro guard.

Before we had done anything toward reorganizing our companies and establishing our line, the rebs had advanced and opened fire. We were ordered up to the breastworks just as we were; and the battle was renewed in earnest, as the rebs were determined to recapture the breastworks and the cannon. They made five different charges during the day.

It was not only a desperate struggle, but it was literally a hand to hand fight. For much of the time nothing but the pile of logs separated the men. Our men would reach over the logs and fire into the faces of the enemy, or they would stab over with their bayonets. Many were shot and stabbed through the crevices and holes between the logs. Men mounted on the works and with muskets rapidly handed to them kept up a continuous fire until shot down, and then others would take their places.

Several times during the day the rebs would show a white flag and as soon as our fire slackened would jump over in little groups and surrender, but others took their places and the fight was kept up.

It was by these breastworks that the celebrated tree was cut off by bullets. Mr. A. A. Humphrey was at the spot the next day and in comparing it with the Bloody Lane on the Antietam battle field declared that the sight was much more terrible and sickening, for while at Antietam there were a great many dead men lying in the road and across the rails of the torn-down fences and out in the cornfields, here they were several deep and horribly torn and mangled.

Gen. McGowan says that the trenches on the right of the breastworks in the bloody angle had to be cleared more than once, and he tells also about the tree, an oak, 22 inches in diameter, that was cut down by musket balls and fell about 12 o'clock Thursday night, injuring several men in the South Carolina regiment.

There has been a mistaken idea among many about the fife and drum being used in the time of battle for the purpose of drowning the shrieks of the wounded and dying. I think none were ever used for this purpose, and I never heard a shriek from a wounded soldier.

The first effect of a wound is numbness, and the wounded seldom speak above a whisper, which is hard to hear in time of battle. Had you been where I was that day, just in front of a belching battery, with roar of the cannon and the whistle of the bullets about your ears, you would not have needed any

Fourth of July celebration to wake you or to shut out of your ears the sighs of the dying.

I think, also, many are mislead by the expression "rivers of blood." If this could be used of any place, it doubtless could of the Bloody Angle; but yet it is an exaggeration and but little better than a lie to the credulous. Of course, if a number of men were shot in a river or brook, their blood would color the water, but it would not be right to say that the blood flowed to your waist without even mentioning the river. On the land the blood is absorbed by the clothing and the soil as fast as it can run from a gunshot wound; it does not make streams or rivulets along the ground. It is best to state things as they are. A lie, or an exaggeration, never does any good. I may in my narrative say many things hard to believe, but it is only because they are strange. I have not falsified and I have not exaggerated.

As our regiments were all broken up, I saw a number of comrades belonging to my company a few rods to the right. At about 2 o'clock in the afternoon we were ordered to stop firing, while a number of rebels came into our line, and then I thought I would go down and join the comrades. On arriving, however, they had left, and the bullets again began to whistle, so I thought I would go back to the place I had left. As I arrived and thought to turn, a bullet struck me in the right arm near the shoulder, just above the armpit.

This caused a numbness, which felled me to the ground. I did not ask any one to assist me but succeeded in my efforts to crawl on my hands and knees. When I had crawled in this way five or ten rods, my numbness had somewhat worked off. Then I made an effort to walk and succeeded in getting a number of rods. Then two men at the rear assisted me to the hospital, which was about a half mile distant.

The doctors being very busy did not examine my wound and as it bled but little they only tied a cloth around my arm and sent me to the general hospital, which was about two miles away.

There the doctors examined my wound carefully and picked out some pieces of cloth. I asked them where the bullet was, and they replied,

"In the shoulder."

I wanted to know if they were going to try and get it out.

One of them said, "No; you have suffered enough for one day."

I told him my shoulder felt all right, but that I felt very badly in my chest and lungs. He thought that that must be a sympathetic pain, caused by the nerves running from the shoulder to the side, and that it would be all right in a few days. I have always doubted whether he said what he really thought or said these things in order to keep me from being alarmed.

They directed me to a tent where there were a few other wounded men, and a good chance to lie down on the straw.

Now, kind reader, just picture to yourself my condition, how I had been marching all the night before, had been in the charge at daylight without a moment's time to eat, had been exposed to a drizzling rain through the day, and now found myself on a bed of straw, wet, tired, wounded, but not hungry, for the bullet had taken all hunger away.

> Sing not to me in the minor key,
> For my flesh is tired and wounded to-night;
> Give me but a ray of that heavenly day,
> Turn sadness to joy my soul to delight.

How glad a poor soldier would be to be at home at such a time and to have the care of those who love him! In the hospital, though the nurses are kind, yet they have so much to do and so many to care for and it becomes so much of a business to them, that they cannot come around very often and they do not wish to fuss with a fellow very much and humor him in some of the little things he likes, and so take it all in all I call it poor care in comparison with what home would give.

I wet my handkerchief and put it on my side and lay down on the bed of straw but I couldn't sleep. I heard the cannons roaring until nearly midnight, but after that I think I slept a little.

The next morning, May 13, 1864, I wrote in my diary as follows.

"At the hospital about two miles from the fight. Had a hard night of it. (Rainy.) Had a hard day to-day. Hard for me to breathe."

CHAPTER VIII.
HOSPITAL EXPERIENCES.

Orders had been given to move the sick and wounded to Fredericksburg. That meant dreary nights and days for me.

On the morning of the 14th of May we were to start. I inquired how far it was, and was told twelve miles. Then they asked me if I would ride in an ambulance.

Fearing the jar of the ambulance would be too much for me, I concluded to walk. As I had rested somewhat and the wound was not bleeding enough to weaken me, and being used to walking, I told them that I thought I would walk part way at least and then if I gave out I would take the ambulance. But they said that if I walked at all, I would be obliged to walk all the way as the ambulance would be full when it overtook me and then, if I gave out, I would be left in a rebel community. But I concluded to run the risk.

I threw away a good pair of boots, which had been sent me from home in a box and took a pair of shoes because they were lighter. Then I tore off the ragged bottoms of my pants up to about the knees, in order to get rid of the weight of mud hanging to them. (Old soldiers will remember how the Virginia mud used to stick to every thing.) And then I started out, independent of my knapsack, haversack, canteen and all other equipments of war.

I thought at first that I would take my canteen, so I could have a drink of water on the road, but finally I gave it up, as too heavy for me to carry. I do not remember eating anything whatever that morning, nor indeed while I was in that hospital.

There was a captain in the tent with me who had been severely wounded in the head just back of the eye. He laid there perfectly motionless when I went in, just faintly breathing. I suppose they thought from the nature of his wound that he could live but a short time. But he was breathing the next day. I told them before I left that I thought he ought to be taken care of, his lips moistened with water and everything done to save him that could be done. They said that so many others had required attention, and thinking his case hopeless, they had given him little heed, but would do more, for having lived so long already, he might pull through. I left him in that way, and have never heard from him since.

Then I set out for Fredericksburg. I did not feel so very weak, but my side was exceedingly sore, and my breathing laborious. I wet my handkerchief and kept it on my side. Having to be careful at every step, I found it a very slow pace that I was able to take. Others went by me, almost as though I was standing still. It did not seem possible for me to travel more than five or six miles.

It was a number of miles before we came to the main road. The walking was rough and muddy. In some places a corduroy road, had been built. Such a road is formed of logs laid side by side across the roadway in marshy spots, and is so called because its surface is rough or ribbed like corduroy. This, when made in haste, as it always was by an army, with varying sizes of logs and without any kind of smoothing down, would be exceedingly rough. You can imagine what it would be to ride over it.

And now, kind reader, I am going to tell what seemed to me the hardest and most cruel thing about the whole war; but I don't know as there was any way to avoid it. Just think of the poor men who had been severely wounded; their wounds after two or three days would partially heal up and then be so sensitive that if the men were at home they would not want any one to come into the room and look at them, or even put a hand on the bedstead; but these poor wounded soldiers were loaded into ambulances and carried from five to fifty miles over just such rough and racking roads, as I have described. It was awful. I was on a piece of corduroy road when an ambulance passed me. It was enough to make one's blood run cold to hear those poor fellows shriek and moan, as they were jolted up and down over those logs. And when the wagon left the corduroy, it would often drop into a mud slough that would almost overturn it.

Those were sounds that I will never forget. I could truly say that I thanked the Lord that he had spared me from such a fate and had given me strength enough to creep or crawl, instead of having to ride.

I have no doubt but that thousands died, who would have lived, if they had not been subjected to such an ordeal.

Oh, this cruel, cruel war! Can the nation ever pay for this untold suffering? Never! Never!

Going on I came to a place where those on foot were taking as a short cut a path across a bend in the main road and saving a considerable distance. So I took the foot-path. In about half a mile I came to a little brook over which a tree had been fallen as a bridge for crossing. It would no doubt have been amusing to an observer to have watched me try to get up among the few branches left and get my feet on to the trunk of that tree so that I could walk across it. For some time it was doubtful whether I could succeed or not. But finally, after exercising much patience and perseverance, I succeeded in getting up and in getting across.

Then I began to feel much encouraged that I might reach Fredericksburg that night. And so I toiled on all that day, feeling very badly, but my strength held out wonderfully.

Just at dusk I arrived at the outskirts of the city, where they were making gruel for invalid soldiers. I drank a very little and inquired for the Second Corps hospital. A man said he would go right there with me. But he led me around from street to street, until I began to feel disheartened.

Somewhere between ten and eleven o'clock, however, we arrived at the hospital and I was comforted with the thought of good care now. A man took me up stairs where a few were lying around on the floor. There was an old rickety settee with one arm. I sat down on this.

As there was a small fireplace in the room and my feet were damp and cold, I asked the man if he wouldn't build a fire for me. He said yes, and passed on. I did not see him again until after light in the morning.

How I spent that night I hardly know. Whether I slept or died I cared little then. I know I felt very badly in the morning. When that man came in, I told him that I thought he had not used me just right. He said that if I would stay the next night he would take the blankets of several soldiers that had died and make me up a good couch. But I made up my mind to use all diligence in getting to the boat-landing, which I was told was about fifteen miles away.

As I felt chilly, I went down to the cookroom and warmed myself. Then I went out on the piazza. While there a team came along with nicknacks to give to the soldiers. Although I did not want anything to eat then, yet, thinking that I might need something on the road, I took a little and put it in my pocket.

I saw the hospital steward, with whom I was acquainted, and told him how I was wounded and about my walking there. He said, if I would ride, he would get me a chance in one of the best ambulance in the army. Afterward, when I saw how good the roads were, I found I would have done well to have accepted his offer, but from the experience of the day before I did not dare to try it.

I told the steward, however, that I would like a little medicine, as I felt very badly. He pointed out the way to the doctor's office. I went there and got me some medicine. Though I could not taste well, yet from its effect I made up my mind that it was a mixture of morphine, whiskey and milk.

It at any rate relieved my distress, and gave a kind of numb feeling. I felt very much as I suppose a stump would feel trying to walk.

It was a splendid morning. Although I could see that it was going to be hotter than the day before, yet I had good courage and was confident that if my strength held out I should reach the steamboat landing in good season.

I walked steadily along until well into the afternoon, when I saw a shower coming up. A little back from the road were some soldiers in a tent. I thought I would go over there and wait until the shower had passed. When I arrived I told them that I wanted to lie down while I waited.

They said, "Come right in. We have a bed all made for you. We saw you coming and have got together all the blankets we have, and now there is a bed for you almost a foot thick."

"You are the tiredest looking man I ever saw," said one of them.

I asked them to awaken me when the shower was over, and lay down. This I called good usage compared with what I received the night before on the old rickety settee. I think the soldiers belonged to the Heavy Maine Artillery.

I fell asleep immediately, and when the shower was over they came and awakened me. I got up. They said they had tried to arouse me before, but I had turned over and said I didn't want to get up then. They thought I didn't understand and so tried it again.

They had built a fire and were making some coffee and were very urgent for me to stay and have some supper with them. I told them that I had no appetite to eat or drink, and I must arrive at the boat landing that night. Thanking them heartily for their great kindness to me and inquiring the distance, I resumed my journey at my very best pace and with increased courage.

The shower had not been very heavy, and so the roads were not very bad, while the air was much cooler, and that helped wonderfully.

I arrived at the landing a little after dark. Seeing a few soldiers around an old shanty, I went up and found that they were making gruel and other light foods for the boys. I got a drink of gruel and then went down to the landing. The boat had arrived and was being unloaded. But this took until after eleven o'clock that night.

When we embarked, all who could walk were ordered to go up on deck. As I had no blanket, a comrade who was convalescing from the measles offered to share his with me, and so we lay down on the hard floor together and tried to get a little sleep. Later on I awoke feeling very chilly. I got up and went down to the lower deck. Up over the boiler, which was a little higher than the floor, I found a warm spot, and there I lay down and went to sleep again.

But when I awoke the next time I could hardly tell whether I was dead or alive. My lungs being so inflamed, the heat from the boiler had seemed to strike all through me and stuff me up. With a big effort I managed to get to the side of the steamer where I could breathe in the cool night breeze, and soon I seemed to feel a little better.

The only place I could then find for a nap was in the space which the doctors had reserved for walking about. But room enough for stretching out at full length was offered me there and I accepted it. A number of times as I lay there I heard some one say, "What is this man here for?" but I didn't let that disturb me.

HOSPITAL EXPERIENCES.

In the morning we came to anchor at Washington. On the wharf was an ambulance waiting to take us to the hospital. Some tables had been set for the soldiers, but we were told that we should get our breakfast at the hospital. Having learned, however, how much promises sometimes amount to, I took a little breakfast then, and got into the ambulance. This time I preferred to ride, for I knew the streets of Washington were smooth and I was very tired.

We had to wait a long time before the ambulance started and then in a short distance we were halted, "to wait for orders," they said. This was repeated over and over, until my patience was nearly exhausted.

It was nearly noon before we arrived at the hospital. This was at Mount Pleasant. Then we had to take a bath and have a change of clothing. All this seemed more than I could accomplish. I was assigned a cot in Ward 2. There I lay down and waited until about 2 o'clock before the warm breakfast was served which had been promised to us early in the morning.

The first night or two the hospital steward awakened me several times telling me that I must not make so much noise as I was disturbing the others. I told him that I would try not to make any noise, but as soon as I fell asleep again I would break my promise.

I soon began to cough up bloody mucous. Then the doctors decided that the bullet was still in my lung.

The doctor in our ward seemed kind, and brought me some medicine which seemed to me to have whiskey in it, although I could not taste distinctly. The next time he came around, I said.

"Doctor, do you order this?"

"No," he replied, "I give this if one wants it."

"Then I don't want it," I said.

"All right," and turning on his heel he went away and never again troubled me with whiskey or other stimulants.

The man who occupied the cot next to mine was wounded across the back of the hand, but not deep enough to injure any of the bones. When he came into the hospital, he appeared quite smart, as though not suffering much from the wound. But he drank whiskey three times a day, and as the wound began to fester the doctor gave him an extra dose to still the nerves so that he might open the sore. The sore continued to gather until it began to be a byword among the comrades.

"Say whiskey to Johnny, and you can do anything to his hand."

The man grew worse. The doctors at length decided that they could not save his life without amputating the hand. This was done, taking it off just below the elbow. But it continued to fester and would not heal, and still the whiskey and the lance were used.

Soon the doctors concluded that the arm above the elbow must be amputated. This was done, but the stump showed no signs of healing. The man kept growing weaker and weaker and could not get off his bed without fainting away. And when I left the hospital, it was not thought that he could live two days. When he entered the hospital I would have swapped my wound for forty like his.

Now, it is my candid opinion that alcohol, before and while in the hospital, was the sole cause of the wound acting as it did. And yet how many will say, alcohol is good in a great many cases. But I believe that with wounds it will prove fatal in almost every instance.

I will now set down a little from my diary, commencing with the second day I was in the hospital, May 17th.

"In hospital. Got a little rested. Got some better care. Coughed up bloody matter. Felt badly. Hope for the best. Got a letter from my wife; so the long day passed."

18th. "In hospital. No particular change. Some hopes of recovery. Feel that the thread of life is brittle at best. Fine weather. Hope on, trust on. The Lord is good, his mercy endureth forever."

19th. "Wrote Mary to come. No particular change. One week since I was wounded. Who could have told that I would have lived until now? The arm seems to be doing well and my lungs as well as could be expected."

My wife did not arrive until June 1st. As she was young and unused to travelling her folks had tried to dissuade her from coming.

Thus the long days and wearisome nights passed slowly away. The doctors told me I could have any kind of food I wanted; so I ordered a custard, but every time some excuse was made and at last I got all out of patience. It was easier to make excuses than to make custards, I found. The night my wife came I would not eat my supper. I think the food was not fit for the sick, such as cold meat and bread, much better suited for well people than for the sick and wounded.

One comrade had such a dinner brought to him, when he was so very low, that he died before dark.

Many kind ladies of the city came into the hospital with tarts and little delicacies to tempt the appetite. They would inquire of the steward who was deserving, and I invariably got something. I would lay it by, and then they would ask,

"Aren't you going to eat it?"

"No, not until mealtime," I would reply.

I noticed that the others ate theirs as soon as handed to them, which I thought a very bad practice.

I am not a believer in dreams, but I had one while in the army, which was very peculiar. I dreamed of being in a large assembly and being hungry. I tried to find something to eat. I thought I found something and began eating, but, Oh! what a horrible taste! I looked to see what I had taken it from, and found it was a coffin and I had been eating a piece of a corpse. I thought my wife was there somewhere and I should find her and go home with her.

When I began to expectorate from the lungs, it tasted to me exactly as it had in my dream.

I told my dream to some in the hospital. They said that they would not be worried about it. I told them that I called it a good dream, for I believed that I should be able to go home with my wife.

One day I asked the doctor if he would allow me to sit up. He said I had better not, but might be bolstered up in my bed. I had already been around the ward almost every day, when he was out, but thought I would ask him to see what he would say.

It was all I could do to walk without staggering and the nurses would be all ready to catch me, if I should fall. One day I went out into the shade, but I think it was doing too much.

As the weather was growing hotter, we decided that I had better go back home to Maine. It seemed like a great undertaking, for the doctor was not at first willing to give his consent; but after much persuasion I obtained a furlough for Maine.

"While here a stranger far from home,
Affliction's waves may round me foam;
And, though like Lazarus, sick and poor,
My heavenly mansion is secure,
I'm going home, I'm going home."

Which home I should reach first, no one could tell.

CHAPTER IX.
MY NATIVE HILLS.

The first of July we started for home, just at night. I walked to the depot. Another comrade who could walk faster than I went ahead and agreed to engage berths in the sleeping car for my wife and me. But when he got there two berths were all he could get. He said he could go in one of the other cars better than I, and he would not take the berth from my wife. He insisted, and I yielded very reluctantly. I did not see him again on the train. But on making inquiries some years afterwards, I learned that he did not recover from his wound.

I saw another man who had a bullet shot through his lungs, and on removing the plaster from the wound he could breathe through the hole.

While on the cars we received many kind attentions from the passengers. One man paid what we had to pay extra for the sleeping car.

We stayed in Boston one day to rest. Arriving at Farmington, we went to my uncle's, Mr. N. Davis. My brother came down and carried us to Phillips the Fourth of July, 1864.

I will leave the reader to imagine how grateful and thankful a person must feel after passing through such scenes and sufferings, to get home once more.

I stood the journey well and felt better than when I started. I was quite comfortable in walking or riding short distances, so I visited relatives and friends.

Nothing unusual took place until along in September, when I coughed up a piece of bone, a picture of which is herewith given. It was a very sharp pointed piece of bone. Not long after this I coughed up a piece of blouse, which is likewise shown.

This seemed to locate the ball without any doubt in the right lung.

My health was exceedingly poor, and with a cold winter coming on the prospect was not very promising. Yet I tried to keep up good courage.

One day a Mr. Whitney came in. He had been trying to get some one to take his place as toll-collector at the North Turner Bridge. Without much seriousness I said that I would go. He replied that he had been thinking of me. Then I told him that I really could not do it; but he answered that my wife could go out and take the toll when I was not able to do it.

As I was drawing no pay from the Government then, I needed some means of support and so this was a chance that I could not afford to lose and I told him I would take it.

This was in October. We went to Farmington on the first day. On the second day I had quite a severe hemorrhage, but continued on my journey until I arrived at North Turner Bridge.

In the evening the directors of the bridge company called and wanted to know if I was the man who was to tend the bridge. I told them I was. They said it was one of their rules that a man should give bonds. I said that I had not been so informed, but could move right out if they wanted me to.

They saw Mr. Whitney, and he told them that they couldn't get a more honest man to tend the bridge, and nothing more was said about the bonds.

I gained quite rapidly from my hemorrhage, and, having been transfered from the Washington to the Augusta hospital, in a few days reported there in person and stayed about two weeks. Then I got a furlough home.

During the winter nothing unusual happened. But in March I had another hemorrhage, which came on very suddenly and was very severe. This time I coughed up a piece of shirting, the largest piece shown in the accompanying picture. As the attack did not last long, I was soon able to be about again.

This spring I bought the tavern stand at the bridge and moved in. Late in the spring I reported again in person at the hospital in Augusta and remained there about two weeks. While I was there one comrade hung himself. I was discharged and returned home.

While we were living at the tavern stand this spring of '65, the school of the district was taught by Laura Lovell, who lived in the same district. She was a lady of good ability, pleasant and courteous. But there was another girl in the district who wanted the school and this caused some feeling. After the school had kept a few weeks, some one said that the supervisor was coming into the school, that it was not profitable, and that the teacher was to be turned out. I had heard that in the past a number of schools had been given up because of similar troubles, but, having so recently moved into the neighborhood, I didn't want to take sides in the trouble. But they were insistent that all should be at the meeting to be held about the matter. So I concluded to go.

When the ball was set to rolling, I could see that they were all on one side and that was the wrong side, for they justified the scholars and threw all the blame on the teacher.

When they had finished and had made out a very strong case against the teacher, some one asked if I had anything to say. I replied that I would like to ask a few questions. Permission being freely given, I asked the teacher if she had had any trouble at the commencement of the school.

"No," was the answer.

"Did you have any difficulty in regard to the lessons?"

"No, not any."

"Who first broke the rules of the school?"

She answered that it was the large scholars of whom there were four or five larger than herself.

"Could you have governed the others?"

"Yes, I have no doubt of that," she replied.

Then I turned to the accusers and asked, "What do you propose for the teacher to do, whip those large scholars into obedience, or what would you require of her?"

No answer was given.

Then the supervisor took it up, asking one young man what his object was in breaking the rules of the school and many other hard questions, to which he would give no answer.

I could see by the looks of the men that they were getting uneasy. The father of the boy who had just been questioned jumped up and said,

"You will have no more trouble from my children. If they make any more trouble, I will take them out of school."

The supervisor talked with the teacher, and let her go on with the school; and at its close we could all truly say that she had kept a very fine school.

Now every one should think soberly before deciding any important question. Let a parent realize how hard it is to manage three or four children, all one family, then think what it must be to have twenty or thirty from different homes, all ready to become jealous with the thought that the teacher may be partial, and all heard and fostered at home when they bring their versions of a school matter, for "our children never tell lies."

Many, many scholars have been taken out of school and their education spoiled without any good reason, just because of some little jealousy or spite that has no good ground for it whatever.

Fathers and mothers, and children, think! think carefully and speak carefully; encourage the teacher, and most schools will be good.

We stayed in the tavern one year. My health was very poor all the time. Once or twice I was confined to the house one or two weeks. In the spring of 1866 I sold out and went to North Turner. I was so as to be around the house all summer but had to sleep in my chair most of the time.

Late in the fall or the first of the winter I had another severe hemorrhage. I had asked Dr. Garcelon of Lewiston, what was good for these hemorrhages and he had prescribed spirits of turpentine, a teaspoonful at a time. I took it as directed, straight. For a little while afterward I felt pretty sick, but it stopped the hemorrhage and that is what I took it for.

Along the middle of winter I was so I could ride out a little. In the last week of January I had another very severe attack of hemorrhage, bleeding twice or three times a day. My lungs seemed to fill up with clots of blood and I would keep expectorating large mouthfuls of it. As soon as my lungs were relieved of the clots, they would bleed again. I had a spittoon which held over a pint. This would fill in a very few minutes. At times the blood would come so rapidly that I would nearly strangle. In about three weeks I had bled more than it seemed possible for one person to bleed and still live.

I coughed up two more pieces of clothing and also, at about the same time, another piece of bone, three quarters of an inch in length. (See picture which is not full size.) This bone I came near losing, as I coughed it up while bleeding and it fell into the spittoon, but the nurse who sat up with me heard it rattle on the bottom and recovered it.

Although it was very cold weather during the three weeks mentioned, right in the dead of winter, the last of January and the first of February, still I could not have any fire in my room, and had to have two watchers. While one was fanning me with overcoat and mittens on, the other sat in the kitchen to get warm. I sat in my chair with my head, side and back packed in wet cloths; and when they took a cloth from off my side it would steam as though taken from a hot stove. But lay it on the chair, and it would soon be frozen stiff.

Most of the time we kept a door open into an unfinished room and occasionally the window in my room. The wind from the fan felt like summer breezes. My pulse remained about 130, and the doctor was giving me medicine all the time to reduce it.

I should not wonder if many on reading this account would discredit it, thinking that it could not be true. As I look back upon it, it seems miraculous to myself.

A man who lived in Turner before I moved there had seen an account in the papers of what I had suffered and how I had coughed up pieces of bone and of clothing and had flatly said that such a thing could not be true and the man live. But one day I happened to meet him in the store when I had been out riding and had been taken with a hemorrhage and had been obliged to stop for medicine. When the man saw me and heard my story he said he should take it all back. He believed it was true.

But during my serious sickness there was only one who entertained hopes of my recovery. That was my only sister. She told the doctor that she thought I would recover.

"How can it be possible!" he exclaimed.

She said that I had recovered from so many bad spells, she believed I would from this also. She is the only one now living who was a constant attendant on me at that time. Her address is Mrs. N. S. Whitman, Lewiston, Me.

I have had many dispute these facts right to my face, saying that my story was impossible, for if a person had a hemorrhage from the lungs to the amount of a spoonful, he would be very weak if not entirely prostrated.

PICTURE OF BONE AND FOUR PIECES OF CLOTH.—See page 87.

I would ask them where the blood did come from; and they would reply, "From the stomach." Then I would ask, "Does any one cough up blood from the stomach, unmixed with food?"

I knew that my stomach was all right, excepting for the inflammation necessarily connected with the fever that was in the system.

After coughing up the two pieces of cloth and the piece of bone, I began to improve. The fever abated, and I began soon to have a fire, in my room. After two or three weeks I could lie down nights in my bed, and then the gain was more rapid.

In June I was able to go to Phillips on a visit. The last of August I returned home and then moved to Turner Village, where we stayed through the winter, and I was able to be about most of the time.

All the while we were at North Turner we failed to get my pension established. Some advised us to call on the town for help, but with the assistance of good friends and by practicing the strictest economy we managed to get along. When at length the pension did come it was only eight dollars a month. But the next year it was increased to twenty-five dollars a month.

The man who wrote the application said that I was "dragging out a miserable existence." He was a very healthy, robust man, a deputy sheriff, and has been dead these twenty years, while I am stilling "dragging out that miserable existence,"—and yet not miserable, for while the body suffers, the mind may enjoy good things. "In this world ye shall have tribulation," but "in me ye shall have peace." In this strong confidence I have rested, "for in him we live and move and have our being." In health, strength and a good constitution there is no surety of life. Many do I know, now dead a long time, with whom a few months before I would have been glad to have exchanged conditions.

In the spring of '68 we moved back to North Turner Bridge. I was then able to be around, but not able to work.

In the spring of '69 we bought a place near the toll house. There I was confined to the house for several months.

In '70 or '71 I was appointed postmaster. As the office was small and the work not hard, with the help of my wife, I managed to get along until '74, although subject to several hemorrhages and being prostrated a part of the time.

About this time the report went out that I had regained my health and had gone into business, and my pension was cut down to fifteen dollars a month. We then had five children and it was only by the strictest economy that we could keep from getting very heavily in debt. After two or three years I succeeded in having my pension increased to twenty-four dollars a month.

All sorts of uncharitable stories were told about me by either those who did not know the facts or were hard toward me for some reason or other. One French woman accused me of picking my teeth to make folks think that I bled at the lungs.

In the latter part of the summer I sold out my place.

Before we moved I must mention an incident that took place between myself and one of the neighbors. We were on very intimate terms of friendship. One night he came home, under the influence of liquor, and ordered his wife to go some little distance to a neighbor's house for some water. She being rather timid, came to our house. We advised her to go to her father's a little further on, but she refused, thinking that her father and her husband would have trouble. My wife went out and got one of the men of the vicinity to go down to the house and look after the drunken man, for fear that he would injure the baby that had been left behind in the cradle.

That man kept watch a while on the outside, but did not see or hear anything unusual, and so at length went off home.

Along in the night we heard a heavy rapping on the kitchen door. I answered it by asking what was wanted. The man wanted to know if his wife was there. I told him that I did not know, as I had not seen her since she went home. He insisted on my getting up to see. I told him that I could not. He went away, and I fell asleep.

Soon my wife came and awakened me saying that the man was getting in at a window. I got up as quick as I could and went to a neighbor's for help, at the same time the wife went up stairs and hid.

As the man had a lantern he searched the lower part of the house and then went up stairs, continuing his search. After a little he discovered where his wife and my wife were hiding, and was just about to rush upon them, when his wife with great presence of mind said in a calm voice,

"Let us go home," and suiting the action to the word, started out.

As they were going down the stairs, she remarked that her wraps were in the kitchen; he went into the kitchen, they escaped him, by turning to the door that led to the street. I was just then returning with the neighbor, whom I had called. The women rushed past us, and then the husband came up in pursuit. He commenced to strike and kick at me, but by dodging and with the help of the old man with me, and also of his son who came up, I managed to escape receiving any of the blows. The son was a large, stalwart man and putting his hand on the drunken man's shoulder marched him off home, where at length he sobered off.

The next morning I had an attack of hemorrhage and was quite poorly for several days.

I did not see my drunken neighbor for a day or two. Then he sent word that he would like to have me come over and see him. I replied that I thought it was his place to come and see me. In about four days I sent a load of goods to Phillips, to which town we were then moving. He came over and said that he never felt so badly in his life as he did when he saw that load of goods start away. He earnestly asked my forgiveness, and said that when they told him what he had done, he could hardly believe it was possible.

I told him that I hoped it would never be repeated, and he declared that it never should be, and he promised me then and there never to touch a drop of liquor as long as he lived. Whether he kept his promise or not, I do not know surely, but I never heard of his being drunk again.

Dear reader, you can see how a kind, tender-hearted friend can be turned into a demon, for no other cause than the power alcohol has over him. Others are transformed into silly foolish fools. And with this latter sort a great many thoughtless men and boys like to have sport,—they enjoy such quaint sayings as this:—

A man named David read on the pipes in a store "T. D." and said it meant "Take it David."

But whether the drunkard rages or laughs, there is no quietness of mind or honor of manhood. It always disgusts me to see one in such an idiotic state.

While men cry out for liberty to eat and drink what they please, I can say,—

Oh! liberty, how hast thou destroyed the children of men! Under thy name have millions been slain both in soul and body, and in thy name millions more will go down to everlasting night.

We declare our independence, but we had better feel our dependence upon God and his Holy Word, and put away the evil of our doing and banish the accursed thing from our land.

MY NATIVE HILLS.

Who hath babblings? Who hath woes?
He that oft to the bottle goes.
Destruction is there: it lurks in the cup;
You're surely slain, if it's not given up.
Wine is a mocker, strong drink a curse,
Deceiving the foolish; oh! what could be worse!
Lead a drunkard's life? Stop and be wise,
If you would escape the redness of eyes;
Even as a serpent's deadly bite,
The adder stings their lives to blight.
A very little now and then
Has led to ruin the sons of men.
If the Good Book they always sought,
They'd touch or taste or handle not.
To young and old that Book will be
A guide that points unerringly.
The sot must be (Oh! think and read:)
The moderate drinker gone to seed.
I've heard men say, they scorned the thought
Of ever becoming a drunken sot:
This did not keep them,—Alas! they fell
To a drunkard's woe, a drunkard's hell,
"Old man," say you? "That's too severe."
I want to help you now and here;
I am your friend; I want to save
You from a drunkard's shameful grave.

After my family had gone to Phillips, I stayed a few days to settle up the business of the postoffice: and then, bidding good-bye to many friends with whom we had spent many pleasant hours, both in business and in social life, I started for my old neighborhood in Phillips.

Now we are once again in the pleasant valley of the Sandy River, where the speckled beauties abound, and where I had as a boy passed some very happy hours in the gay sports of boyhood.

CHAPTER X.
WAITING.

During the winter of 1874-5 we lived a half of a mile from the school house, and boarded a young man who attended the school that he might take the children back and forth, as I was not able to do that and take care of the out of door chores.

I soon learned from the children that they had an old-fashioned teacher, one who could enjoy an old-fashioned spelling school. And before long the spelling schools of that district were a theme of daily conversation, and soon other districts caught the enthusiasm, and there were spelling matches before crowded houses.

Many were the gay scenes in connection with them. It made the old people feel young again. The spelling was interspersed with singing, dialogues and declamations, and on the closing night a friendly paper was introduced, and my eldest daughter was selected to read the paper. Here my services were requested, and I took the part of adding some poetry touching off the peculiarities of the different members of the school. For example,—

> There is Francis Lufkin, to chatting he's inclined,
> Just give him a chance, and he'll talk you quite blind;
> In asking of questions he's always around;
> In hair and whiskers he always abounds.

Our boarder said that there should not be anything in the paper about him, and so he was very watchful when she was reading it over. I suggested that she had better read it over once in the parlor in the same loud tone that she would use at the school house. She did so, and he followed around to the front of the house and listened through the window. Of course she omitted the part that bore on him. It ran as follows:

> There's Eliab Chandler, whose hair is so curly;
> You just cross his track, he'll look pretty surly.
> He talks quite loud, but never roars;
> He thinks more of the girls than of doing the chores.

Being of a sensitive nature, he was taken down very much, to the great delight of his schoolmates. The teacher was pleased with the moral tone, sentiment and fun, as were all the rest. And thus ended one of the best spelling schools I ever attended.

In the spring of 1875 I purchased a place in West Phillips, three-quarters of a mile from Madrid, but did not move until the first of May. For three or four years my health permitted me to go around and enjoy the society of the vicinity, which I call very good. We had a religious meeting quite regularly, and also a Reform Club, which was shared in by our best citizens, and a crowded house was the invariable rule at its exercises. The programme consisted of prayer, singing, questions, signing the pledge, and reading a paper, and quite often we had a lecture from some good speaker.

In this manner a few years glided by, while I was a sufferer yet able to enjoy many of the common blessings of life. About 1879 I was taken down again with severe hemorrhages and confined to my bed. After one year I applied for an increase of pension, which had been but twenty-four dollars a month and totally inadequate for my expenses.

After sending in the application the authorities wished to know how much care I had to have, stating that they could not tell from the doctor's certificate whether I was entitled to thirty-one or fifty dollars a month. The man who did the business for me came to take the evidence. I was too sick at the time to have the depositions taken in my room. After taking my wife's and one small girl's he said that was enough. I should have objected to this if I had known in time. But he ought to have known, as he was quite an eminent lawyer at the time, and has since become a judge.

As might have been expected they only gave me the thirty-one dollars a month. I spoke to the lawyer about it. He said he thought it enough and as much as I ought to expect. I asked him what he would be willing to take my place for. He seemed somewhat indignant and said that he would rather have been killed outright than to have been wounded as I was.

He was probably like many others who did not stop to think how it would be if they themselves were in my place. By the strictest economy I could not help getting into debt, so that when pay day came, I could only pay about half of what I was owing.

One time I sent by my son about half of what I owed the storekeeper. He said he thought it strange that I could not pay him all, as I was getting a big pension. He said so much that the boy paid him the whole amount, taking it from other money which I had given him to carry to others that I was owing. Then the storekeeper accused the boy of keeping back the amount which I had sent him. This aroused our indignation somewhat, as the boy had always been faithful and honest.

The storekeeper also said that I was getting as much pay as any common laborer. I was quite sick at the time, but I resolved to write to him, and did so by writing a few lines at a time. I called his attention to these facts to show him the difference between my expenses and those of a common laborer's:

I had a large doctor's bill all the time, while the common laborer usually had none; I had to have a fire night and day, lights all night, and one or two attendants all the time. Even if the attendants were out of my own family, yet in waiting on me they were kept from other work which they might do and so earn something. As this man kept a hotel as well as a store, his wife could be earning by looking after the company, while my wife could do nothing of the kind, and all of her needs had to be supplied from my pension. If any one will give it a little thought, he can easily see the difference between my expenses and those of a common laborer.

I do not write these things with any spirit of accusation or of retaliation, but merely for an explanation. How many times have I heard people say after a few weeks or months of sickness that it had put them back so very much, and yet I had had years of sickness. While I did not expect to be paid for my suffering, I thought I ought to have the common comforts of life. A number of years I drew but thirty-one dollars a month, when by law I was entitled to seventy-two. I had good reason to be grieved at the expression of lack of confidence and begrudging which came from persons who had reaped so many advantages from the services of the wounded soldier. Their property had nearly doubled in value while we had toiled and sacrificed and suffered the hardships of which few can conceive. Our pay had been the small pittance of about five dollars a month in gold. One man said the Government had paid us all it had agreed to, and that that was enough.

Now, kind reader, I will leave it with you, if such sayings are charitable to the poor wounded soldiers. Would you be willing to go, or to have your children go and suffer what we have had to endure for any less reward? But while the fault finders comprise but a small part of the people, I hope that they will see their selfish spirit and act upon the principle of the Golden Rule, "Therefore, all things whatsoever ye would that men should do to you, do ye even so to them; for this is the law and the prophets." There is no way of judging so good and safe, as to put yourself, as far as possible, in the other man's circumstances.

Perhaps you will say that I am too sensitive on this point. But I have had these things to face, and you would feel exactly as I do, if you were in my place. I never knew a sick day until I was wounded, and I have not known a well one since I was wounded; while a crust was relished then more than all the luxuries can be now. Any one who has tried these things, as I have, and has passed from perfect health to perfect invalidism, as I have, will know of what I speak.

Better let your tongue cleave to the roof of your mouth, than to say anything wrongfully of the soldier, who, by his noble service, saved the country from its perilous condition, bringing in a prosperity such as no other nation has ever known. When I see this prosperity, do I regret my part of the service and sufferings? Ah! no.

Some have said it is sweet to die for one's country, but I think that to die for right principles and to help drive such a curse as slavery out of our land should gain praise, not censure; help, not neglect; sympathy, not reproach.

To speak of a pension, should be to call up thoughts of honor for the soldier, for wounds received show that it is an honor dearly bought. I think the poet was right when he wrote these lines:

"Home returning from the fight,
  They win their way with noble scars.
 They point to wounds, by traitors' hands,
  Who fought against the stripes and stars,
 Beautiful stars, beautiful stars,
 Stars of our union, beautiful, beautiful stars."

To speak of the pension as a dishonor is not patriotic. No one can be a lover of his country and reproach its defenders. I will admit that there were a few reckless characters in the army,— indeed, in my story I have told you of several,— and yet to speak of the whole as a set of bummers would be an aggravating sin. The soldier who is honorable should be honored by all. "Honor to whom honor is due."

WAITING.

After I had been confined to my bed for four years I had my pension raised to fifty dollars a month. By practicing economy this was enough for my expenses. A large part of the time I could sit up long enough only to have my bed made, and frequently did not do even that for two or three days. I would gain slowly for two or three weeks and then have a bleeding spell that put me away back again.

Some said that they did not see why I did not get better, but for my part I could not see why I did not die. For about six years I was confined to my bed most of the time. Then I began again to improve and could ride out a little.

In 1881 I was glad that I was not the President of the United States. What a shock the world received when tidings went with lightning rapidity all over it that James A. Garfield had been shot in Washington! I could sympathize with him in his sufferings. I had been wounded in the same way, but I was glad that I was not the President, because in some respects I could insist upon better treatment than was given him as I will proceed to tell.

For days and weeks how we prayed for him! But faith and works must go together, and in my humble opinion works did not go with the prayer of faith. Although they summoned the greatest physicians and surgeons of the land, yet even great men make mistakes.

What! speak against the most eminent men of our land! Yet the foolish may confound the wise. The following considerations make me doubt the treatment. In the first place they probed for the ball where it was not and of course the probe made a path for itself, and that caused another wound. And then they gave him stimulants. I think I have demonstrated in my experience that when the system is excited above its normal condition to give it at that time a stimulant is to do it an injury. When the heart beats above one hundred a minute, then to give a stimulant of any kind is to my mind very harmful.

So, when they gave our beloved President every few hours three spoonfuls of old brandy, which had been sent him by the Queen of England, no wonder he said,

"Doctor, are you not rumming me too much?"

According to my experience this would be very hurtful. A teaspoonful of brandy would immediately injure me. Once my doctor thought he would medicate some brandy and left it for me to take in teaspoonful doses at regular intervals. But I felt that it was injuring me and set it aside. He told me afterwards that it was almost wholly brandy.

You may say that my opinion is worth nothing, but we have doctors who have climbed to the top round in the profession who have proved in all cases of wounds that stimulants are an injury.

And so, my reader, I have come to the conviction that if I had used stimulants even in a very moderate quantity, I should not now be writing to you. I am glad, therefore, to-day that I was not a President.

In 1887 we moved to Phillips village, and there for nearly five years nothing unusual befell me. My health was poor with occasionally a sick spell that brought me to the bed.

In July 1892 my wife was taken sick and after a sickness of one hundred days, during which she was an extreme sufferer, she passed away.

Death did not stay to inquire whether I could spare her, her who had stood over me night and day, lo! these many years, waiting and anxious to do all that could be done, and then when I could get along without her she would sit up with the sick of the neighborhood, no matter how hard she had worked or whether it was a special friend or not. I can truthfully say that she always did more than her part. While others made excuses, she would make none. So I and many others have good reason for thanking God for giving her a heart and hand to sympathize and care for the sick and suffering.

One night during her sickness we failed to get some one to care for her, and some had made small excuses. I said to her, "Mary, you did not make such excuses."

She answered, "I am not sorry for what I have done for others."

Thus it will be with you and me, for the Great Judge will say in that day, "As ye have done it to the least of these my brethren ye have done it unto me." May it be our happy lot to have no regrets at the last.

In a conversation with her, she said that she did not fear to die, but she only feared that I would be neglected. But, bless the Lord! my wants have all been supplied marvelously through His care. But though other friends arise to care for you, how you miss the loved ones who have gone before! Although everything is done by doctors, nurses and friends, yet all in vain,—we miss her.

My health was so that I could be about. My pension was cut down two or three years before to thirty dollars a month. That made it hard for me, but still I got on.

In October 1893 I was again attacked with hemorrhages, but I kept about until January 3, 1894. Then I was confined to my bed, and soon la grippe came on me also. In May and June I gained a little. In July I had another hemorrhage lasting several days. Since that time up to the present I have had five or six hemorrhages, and have coughed up consider-able corrupt matter, showing that the lung must be in a decayed state.

CHAPTER XI.

A GREAT DISCOVERY—THE WONDERS OF THE X-RAY.

On the 17th of April, 1897, I met Prof. W. C. Strong of Bates College, Lewiston, Maine, for the purpose of having the ball in my lung located by means of the X-ray. Those present were my sister, Mrs. N. S. Whitman, my niece, Mrs. Retta Newman, my nephew, Mr. Emerson Whitman, Dr. Aurelia Springer and others. We were taken into a dark room where we remained for some time to render our eyes sensitive to faint light. We were surprised to find that, in a room which at first appeared almost totally dark, our sight became so keen that all the objects in it were clearly seen. All who were present except myself saw the ball plainly by the aid of the fluoroscope; and at a later examination, I was able to do the same by the aid of a mirror so inclined as to reflect the light to my eyes. Dr. Springer especially took careful note of the position of the ball. A week later, the Professor made two photographs of the ball and the surrounding parts of my body, and, still later, carefully identified the location of the ball in the lung. Here is what Professor Strong says:

"It has often been said that the remarkable discovery of the X-ray, by which we are enabled, in a certain sense, to look through opaque bodies and see what is inside them, came too late. With the knowledge which we now possess, how many lives might have been saved during the Civil War, how any cases of misapplied treatment might have been avoided, Mr. Wing has lived on for thirty-four years to demonstrate.

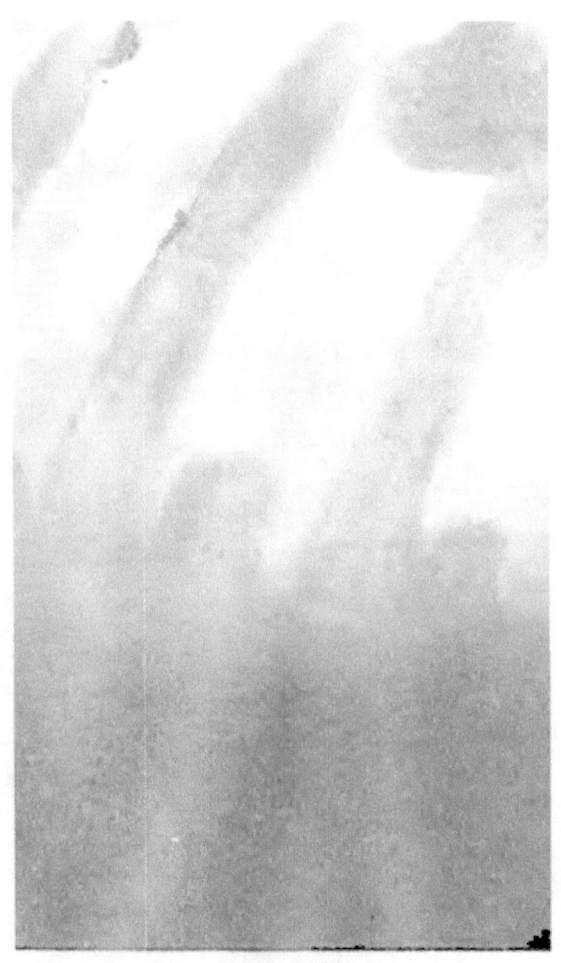

Picture of Ball in its Present Location.

Perhaps the X-ray might have saved Garfield's life. But it is useless to speculate or indulge in vain regrets. In one sense, every new discovery or invention comes too late; it cannot benefit the myriads of suffering humanity who have lived and died before us.

"Mr. Wing came first for X-ray examination on the morning of April 16, 1897. Except for the irritation caused by the presence of the ball in his lung, and the feebleness of enforced inactivity he appeared to be in a very good state of health. Inquiry concerning the bullet failed to elicit any definite information beyond the fact that it was somewhere on the right side. It was evident that he would be better pleased to have the ball located without any definite clew. An X-ray tube furnished by Stanley Bros., of Newton, Mass., was selected for the work. This had seen much use, and the vacuum had become very high so as to emit rays of great penetrating power. The tube was excited by a Stanley double-plate Holtz machine, running at the rate of about 1500 revolutions per minute and capable of giving 8 inch sparks in rapid succession. The room was made as dark as possible, and the tube was inclosed in a light-tight box; the discharge spark was also screened from view. These precautions were taken in order to bring the eye into a very sensitive condition for seeing and are absolutely essential for the best work with the fluoroscope.

"The examination was begun with the subject's back to the tube. A glance showed the position of the clavicle, ribs and vertebral column and disclosed the outlines of the lungs, heart and liver. Low down on the right side, nearly touching the upper border of the shadow of the liver, was observed a dark round spot nearly as large as a silver dollar, which was immediately identified as the enlarged shadow of the bullet. The size of the shadow indicated a bullet of large caliber and a location near the back side of the body. The subject was then turned round so as to face the tube, which was placed opposite the right lung, and the examination was continued over the back. The shadow of the bullet was now more clearly seen, of the size of a bronze penny, perfectly round and sharply defined. A careful study was then made of the precise location of the bullet. It was found practicable to observe the shadow in all positions of the body except those in which the X-rays were cut off by the vertebral column. By a study of the positions of the ribs and by turning the body from side to side so as to change the position of the shadow, the precise location of the bullet was determined with great accuracy. This was found to be in the right lung, opposite the opening between the 8th and 9th ribs, on the back side, about four inches from the line of the vertebral column, and about two inches inward from the surface of the body. It is not probable that the location given is in error more than half an inch in any direction.

"As the fluoroscope examination proved to be somewhat exhausting, the photographic process was deferred till the morning of April 23rd. The patient was then placed on his back over an 8x10 photographic plate, the X-ray tube being fixed about ten inches above the chest and directly over the location of the bullet. Two photographs were taken with exposures of twenty and thirty minutes respectively, the second of which is reproduced in the half-tone engraving on page 105.

"In the photograph, the shadow of the ribs and the vertebrae are distinct because they were stationary and near the photograph plate, while the shadow of the upper edge of the liver is indistinct because it was moving up and down at each act of respiration. The shadow of the bullet, too, loses its roundness because of the movement of the lung, a fact which the fluoroscope examination amply confirms. Most curious perhaps of all, are the two fragments of the bullet lodged in the 7th and 8th ribs, and the piece of bone broken out of the

7th rib, which appears to have been the source of the bone fragments coughed up by the patient.

"That the bullet is in the substance of the lung is unquestionable; it moves with the lung; its shadow is distinctly separated from that of the liver and contiguous diaphragm. Such has always been the view of Mr. Wing and of reputable physicians who have attended him. But how its location as low down as the 9th rib, or how the fracture of the 7th rib and the lodgment of fragments of the bullet in the 7th and 8th ribs are consistent with the location of the bullet in the lung, or with the entrance through the shoulder and above the arm pit, the writer does not attempt to explain. Perhaps the body was inclined to the right, the arm being raised at the moment of receiving the bullet, which may also have been fired from above. Perhaps the impact of the bullet on the ribs may have resulted in a rebound into the lungs. The bullet is evidently a spherical one of large size, and seems to be such as was formerly used in the old fashioned Springfield rifle. That a bullet of such size and weight could be carried for thirty-four years in the delicate tissues of the lungs has been thought by some impossible. Of the fact, however, there can be no longer any doubt. Similar cases must be extremely rare."

Professor Strong's description of the finding of the ball by means of the X-ray will be interesting and profitable, if studied with care. The engraving on page 111, was made from the photograph taken by him. There, at last, is revealed the object which has caused all my sufferings, and which has been in motion with every breath for thirty-four years.

It is my opinion that as the lung has suppurated the bullet has lowered from its first position two or three inches, leaving a cavity along its path. Almost every day I have expectorated something showing decay and causing hemorrhage, and to-day I am suffering from the same cause. Another reason for thinking that the ball has lowered is that I can take a longer breath than formerly.

For the first few years after I was wounded, my breath was quite short and I could not increase it even a little without feeling an injury. There must be cavities in my lung because the blood clots have often been so large that I could not cough them up, but had to wait for their resolution. Had the X-ray been applied when I was wounded, I might now present facts in this connection instead of suppositions, though the theories I have proposed are quite satisfactory.

On the page opposite is the cut of the X-ray apparatus used. Prof. Strong will describe the methods of using it and tell something about the discovery of the X-ray and what they are. Here is what he says: "Early in 1896, Prof. Roentgen of the University of Wurtzburg, Bavaria, announced to an incredulous world that he had discovered a new kind of radiance, which would produce photographic effects through opaque objects, and also render some bodies fluorescent, or self-luminous. The idea of photographing, and especially of seeing, through a thick plank took hold instantly of both the scientific and unscientific mind, and set a multitude of experimentors at work on both continents. The wonder grew into a craze, and still the wonder grew. The results are too well-known to need comment here, but a few words about apparatus and methods may not be out of place.

"The source of the X-rays is some form of a glass bulb, known as a crooks or X-ray tube, in which has been produced, by exhaustion of the air, a very high vacuum. Within the bulb are two metal plates, or poles, known as the anode and the kathode, a little distance apart and variously arranged, the same being connected with the outside by platinum wires passing through the glass. Through the bulb and from the anode to the kathode, are discharged, at a very rapid rate, sparks of electrictity, which may be consideræred flashes of

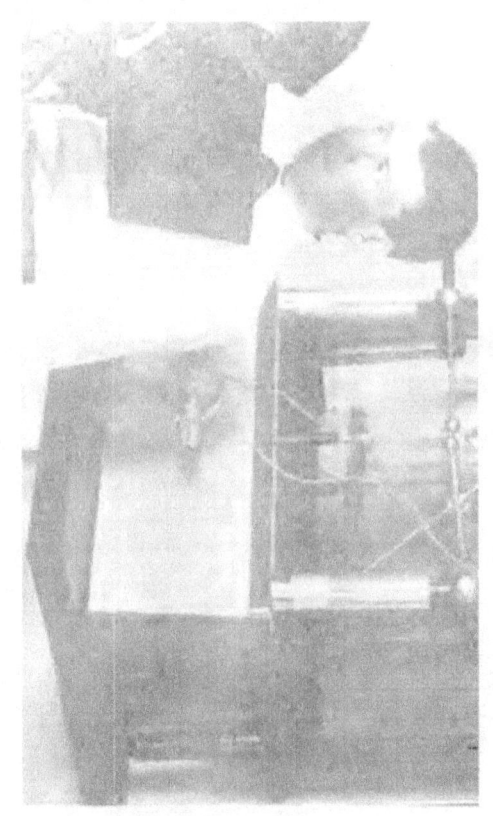

lightning on a small scale. A peculiar radiance is thus set up which proceeds in straight lines from the kathode and is known as the *kathode rays*. Any object on which the visible kathode rays fall becomes the source of the invisible X-rays, which have excited so much interest. The X-rays pass through some bodies more readily than through others. Wood, flesh, and most organic bodies are more or less transparent to them, while metals, bones, and other dense bodies are more or less opaque. Hence, if these rays pass through the human body, the bones and other dense structures are revealed by their shadows. It should be remembered that these rays do not illuminate objects like ordinary light; they do, however, affect photographic plates and render fluorescent or self luminous a large number of bodies, of which calcium tungstate is one of the most remarkable. A piece of cardboard coated with the last named substance is called a *fluorescent screen*, and an instrument for using such a screen, in a dark chamber at a suitable distance from the eye, is called a *fluoroscope*. The outlines of the bullet in Mr. Wing's case were seen as a shadow in the fluoroscope, because the bullet stopped the X-rays while surrounding parts of the body permitted them to pass through. The method of use is well illustrated by the cut on page 111. The X-ray tube is connected by wires with a Stanley X-ray machine, which is powerful enough to discharge itself rapidly through a space of eight inches between the poles. The X-ray tube is placed at one side of the body while the observer at the other side examines the shadows by means of the fluoroscope. If a photograph is desired, the photographic plate, shielded from light, takes the place of the fluoroscope and the observer.

"What the X-rays are is not certainly known. They are probably related to light as a part of a very extensive series of waves in the universal ether, differing from one another simply in wave breadth. Out of this vast series, several other kinds of waves also do not produce visible effects, — for example, the radiations of electricity, of heat and of actinic energy. A number of other kinds are distinguished by the colors which they produce, those which produce a red color being about twice as broad as those which produce a violet. To view the matter from this standpoint, it is scarcely less wonderful that the X-rays should pass through objects opaque to light, than that the heat waves should do the same, a fact which has long been known. The weight of scientific opinion is decidedly in favor of the view that the X-rays are the least broad waves of any at present known. Moreover, there are different kinds of X-rays, which seem to form a series among themselves, differing, like the others, it is presumed, in wavebreadth.

CHAPTER XII.

CONCLUSION.

Dear Reader : I have given you the narration of my life as plainly and correctly as it is possible for me to pen it. I have drawn out some thoughts, but I hope you will be able to bring out many more, for precepts, and that you may practice them, that they may be profitable to you and all that may come under your influence.

Some said I preached too much, perhaps so, but the mere facts incident to my life, if they do not preach, I should never have given them to you.

In thinking over the incidents in my life to me have been very pleasant and profitable, and so I hope they will be to you; if I gain nothing more I shall not regret it.

Would you be willing to live your life again, with all of its wearisome days and nights, with death surely so near? Yes, if it would do others good, but not for silver or gold although it be in abundance.

Dear Friends, I call you friends for I do not know that I have an enemy in the world, and although I may never know you personally yet in thought I can see you reading the book with interest and surprise, ready to say, " How can these things be?" Facts are stubborn things, but it is wrong to try to change them.

Let me introduce Mrs. N. S. Whitman.

I am a sister of the author of this book. Will say that I was present when he coughed up the two pieces of cloth, and a piece of bone, the last mentioned, and anyone seeing the hemorrhages, sitting in his chair night and day, with only a quilt around him, side, back and head wet, and someone fanning him most of the time, without fire, in cold midwinter weather, knowing these things, will say he has not represented them any too strong, having read his book I endorse every word.   MRS. NANCY S. WHITMAN.

CONCLUSION.

After this testimony and that of Prof. Strong's if there should be a doubting Thomas I think it would be well for them to keep their doubts to themselves, for not any more testimony will be given.

While in the hospital at Washington, D. C., I left off writing in my diary. That was the 21st day of June, 1864, and I had not seen the book for a number of years. On the 22nd day of June, 1894, I commenced keeping the diary again after an interval of just thirty years. Sometimes we may be directed to commence where we left off. It would be well sometimes to leave off where we commence, for it is sad to connect the links of a downward career.

For over thirty-two years of my life I did not know what a sick day was; and now for more than thirty-four years I have not known a fully well day. Will all these sick days be cancelled and I be free? No.

"And though I give my body to be burned and have not love, it profiteth me nothing."

"So am I made to possess months of vanity, and wearisome nights are appointed to me."

On looking back the years seem "like a tale that is told," and I can say with the Apostle "for our light affliction which is but for a moment worketh for us a far more exceeding and eternal weight of glory."

This brings to my mind the thought that if we sleep in the grave thousands of years, we should not realize that a moment had elapsed. Ah! say you, that is Advent doctrine! But it makes me think of a conversation which I once had with an Advent minister. He told all about what the Lord was going to do very soon. I listened for some time and then remarked that I was not so much concerned about what the Lord was going to do as I was about what Sam Wing was going to do.

If we worry and weep let it be for ourselves, our children, our neighbors and a world lying in wickedness under the condemnation of a guilty conscience and an offended God.

CONCLUSION.

And this is the greatest object of this little book. Not only may you find it pleasant and interesting reading, but a helpful and lasting benefit. If you do not agree with me in some things, yet ponder well what I have written and take from it all the good there may be. "For we know that all things work together for good to them that love God." He has a wise purpose in keeping many things from us in this world, but as much as is necessary for us to know He has plainly told us; and happy is the man who is governed and controlled by His Word.

"For blessed is that servant whom his Lord, when he cometh, shall find so doing." Why will not this be enough? We are like children who are asked to do something and right straight off want to do something entirely different. So instead of doing what the Lord has commanded us, we strive to find out when and what he is going to do. How vexed we oftentimes become with children who will not attend to the things we wish them to!

"Behold to obey is better than sacrifice."

If the many who have assisted and encouraged me in writing this book, to all I feel grateful. Please allow me to make mention of three, — the first my son said "Father, you ought to write your biography." These are but a few words, but it was all the argument that I needed, and never since then have I felt that I ought not to write it.

Prof. A. W. Anthony of Cobb's Divinity School, Lewiston, Maine, who wrote the introduction and gave me help and encouragement, and is entitled to sincere thanks from me and the reader. The service Prof. Strong has rendered as seen in the eleventh chapter, should receive the hearty commendation of all. He has given us the facts and as good an explanation as any one could in so short a space; but as many facts cannot be explained yet when they become familiar they cease to be a mystery, while some try to explain they only add darkness instead of light. While our own life is a mystery, yet when under the trying circumstances truthfully narrated in this book we are ready to exclaim, "Nothing is impossible with God!" but with us nothing is possible only what he may give, and as

CONCLUSION.

he has given this wonderful power, the X-ray and a knowledge to use it we should be devoutly thankful.

Ho, my Comrades! Let me say a word to you, for you know of many of the things of which I have written, as peradventure you may have seen more of army life than I have, yet I hope not more of its consequences or suffering. I feel like taking you by the hand and saying, "Only one more battle to fight, only one more river to cross." The march must be short and victory certain if we follow our captain, for death will be swallowed up in victory. While I remember the many favors and sympathy to me and others, I feel reverently to say, "The Lord bless you."

To the young: To you it has been my greatest desire that this book should benefit. While you may read and know about wars yet the reality I hope you will never know, and peace, prosperity and perpetual harmony be yours forever. You may have many a battle to fight against wrong, but as your day so shall your strength be.

> "Yield not to temptation, for yielding is sin,
> Each victory will help you some other to win."

There are many things I would like to say, but as all things of this world have an end, I will bid you good bye, hoping you will remember the great object of life, and at the last you will have no regrets.

> "To young and old, rich or poor,
> To you I'll say but little more."
> How many will think, when this book is read,
> What I have suffered, what I have said;
> It is all right, and just, and true,
> As I can pen it, I leave it with you
> To think what you may or say what you will;
> In this I am glad my mission I fill.
> When you read this book and no good you find,
> None would feel worse, just bear it in mind
> Than your humble servant, who loves to dwell
> In your kind heart, the story to tell.
> Oh! This is my wish, that while you read
> To every good precept you will give heed,
> And treasure them up, not like the miser,
> For only what we practice will make us the wiser.
> To know very much, and nothing do,
> Will make a fool of me and you:
> For to do my very best I always shall try,
> And now let me bid you a hearty good-bye.

THE END.

FROM PROF. BRACKETT.

Dear Brother: Feeling that you would be glad to do a favor to a soldier, a brother and a friend from boyhood, and also one that has seen much trouble I will pen a few thoughts hoping you will add many more. S. B. WING.

Bro. Brackett's letter follows:

THE TRUTH AS I VIEW IT.

I have been acquainted with Bro. Wing, the author of this book, and with pleasure I endorse it, believing it to be truthful in every particular and detail, and the experiences he has been called to pass through although marvelous and without a precedent yet they should not be doubted when coming from such a source and with such an array of witnesses. For me to doubt Mr. Wing and what I have heard from time to time would be incredulity not justifiable. I also think his book will be profitable and interesting to all, high or low, rich or poor, learned or unlearned, as the facts so clearly point to the power and goodness of God and we can all join with the poet,

> "God moves in a mysterious way
> His wonders to perform,
> He plants His footsteps in the sea,
> And rides upon the storm."

I give the book my unqualified endorsement, hoping as you read, it will point you to the Lamb of God that taketh away the sin of the world. N. C. BRACKETT.

President of Storer College, Harper's Ferry, West Va.

HISTORY
ON THE
WING FAMILY.

Sir Theodore Wing of England, the first Wing that is known,
In the history of Wayne, Maine, this is what is shown:
As far back as four hundred years and more.
He received a knightly Acolade, and therefore
It was an honor from King Henry the Seventh to be,
The pride of old England, so honorable was he.
In the Armory of Great Britain 'tis there you will spy
The Wing Armor and coat of arms and near by
A shield beautifully embossed with silver and green,
And between two wings a silk wreath, so loved, is seen,
These were the richest and best that a King could bestow,
But greater honor and praise did all people show.
Lord and warden of the wastes and liveries was he,
And in true heraldic history, his name we see.
King Henry the Seventh no greater honor could give
Than was given Sir Theodore as long as he lived.
For splendor and beauty, there could not be found one
Arrayed more royally, except the King on his throne.
From him descended the one that to America came,
Married Rev. S. Batchelder's daughter, Deborah by name.
John Wing was honorable, his descendants we claim,
One and all of them to make a beautiful chain.
They came to Lynn, Mass.,—in sixteen hundred thirty-two,
And joined the Pilgrim band as all good people do.
By John Alden and Miles Standish, their land was laid out,
As history speaks of them it gives no room to doubt.
Now in this line in seventeen hundred twenty-two,
Was born one Simeon Wing, and in life quite well to do.
He married Mary Allen, and born to them numbers nine,
Two girls and seven boys, for women and men they were fine.
The oldest married Job Fuller, Elizabeth by name.
They were the first white people that settled in Wayne,
Going for hundreds of miles mostly woods on horseback,
Grappling with cold and Indians—for courage they did n't lack.
And in a few years returning back to their home,

Telling about Wayne—they all concluded to come.
Leaving William, the youngest, with the old folks to stay,
In a short time they were ready and soon on their way.
As they were going by boat when far out to sea,
Then appeared William. Oh, William! yes, surely, 'tis he.
Now on board the boat were six sons of Simeon Wing;
Where's Moses, dear boy?—he ran away from home, poor thing!
These six with the others safely arrived at Wayne pond;
Each farm adjoining the pond they went nearly around.
In the Continental Army there Moses was found;
To fight for home and country it seems he was bound.
How hard for a boy of sixteen, no one could tell all,
There when in a fierce fight he was struck by a ball.
These troubles for a few years (your pardon I beg)
For through his long life he wore a wooden leg;
Discharged seventeen hundred eighty-two at Falmouth, Maine,
Father, mother, brothers, sisters, he soon joined in Wayne.
He became a physician and surgeon of high renown.
His practice reached far and wide into many a town.
Moses Wing in his dealings with men, we all do agree
That he was a Christian; faithful and loyal was he.
His brother William was despondent and could not be roused,
Pushing him suddenly into the pond he was soused.
It is almost miraculous, the story they tell,—
That in a few days he was perfectly well.
No jail-bird scape-grace in Simeon's family was found,
Elizabeth, Thomas, Ebenezer, and Moses, the renowned,
Aaron, Allen, Simeon, Mary, and William comes last,
None of them drunken mad-men and none of them fast.
Moses Wing born seventeen hundred fifty-nine and he
Married Polly Chandler and to them four children you'll see—
Betsey, Moses Jr., Polly, and John, and they motherless,
He married Patty Maxim, their lonesome home to bless.
A relative of Hiram Maxim, who made the best gun,
And his praises are everywhere under the sun.
To Moses' second wife six children were given, but hark!
Without such troublesome comforts this world would be dark!
Dr. Samuel Wing, born seventeen hundred ninety-two,
Florinda, Martha, Mary, Achsah, Pinkney, that must do;
We think of their merits and worthy lives they did live,
Aye, with thousands, our tribute of love freely give.
Dr. Samuel Wing married Mary B. Norcross, they had
Six boys, four girls, a goodly heritage to make them glad.
Jessie, Moses, Enoch, Mary, Silas,—the next five are
Eunice, Samuel, Martha, Nancy, and Norris, there.

Dr. S. Wing was a college graduate and good,
A large practice but he did not follow it as he should,
Having large boys he went to farming to keep them straight,
Let us all agree 'twas nearly right at any rate.
He settled in Phillips, Maine, and there made it his home,
Steady, industrious, he never wanted to roam.
Jesse was a farmer and quite well to do, but then,
If hay was ever so high he'd only take dollars ten.
For honesty, he was an example for one and all.
He had six children, but Rose was the first to fall.
He soon followed her so very demented was he.
But his works and fellowship long remembered will be.
Elizabeth, John, Rose, Morrill, George, and Lewis, the boy
That we'll all long remember with sadness and joy.
Moses was unfortunate in losing his sight,
Oh! how terrible to live in the darkness of night!
He had but one boy, his name was Nathan D. Wing,
And it always cheered very much to hear him sing.
And Enoch, and Mary, were taken while tender in years.
We cannot bring them back with crying or tears!
Silas Maxim Wing, had twelve children, O! how sad!
O, no, only enough to make them happy and glad.
Ida, Ella, Benjamin, Harvey, Bion, Lura, that's half,
Ira, Orra, Abby, Davis, Rose, Lettie, *don't* laugh,
For he has brought them all up,—has something to spare,
Save three who died in youth—most all such sorrows do share.
They are all good and industrious and are well fed.
How it makes people glad to see his cranberry bed.
His orchard with apples, pears, plums, and grapes, to spare.
Strawberries, raspberries, and honey, make a living so rare,
And all in good humor coming around the board,
Surely we can all say, he lives like a lord,
Sometimes fishing, or hunting, is where he is found;
The baying of his dog the hills and valleys resound.
He'll tell you just where he's been, what he saw wild or tame,
And how very nearly he came to getting his game.
Eunice was frail but will be remembered in love.
(No descendants) we trust she is singing above.
Samuel Brackett Wing was called the unlucky child;
He was loved by his mother so gentle and mild.
All along life's flowery pathway many a thorn was strown,
Never complaining but hoping good seed he had sown.
He wrote a little book of what the Lord had carried him through;
History gives nothing like it, sure 'tis something new,
Coughing up four pieces of cloth, and two of bone,

In the history of all nations, of such you'll find none.
A ball in his lung, and located by the X ray—
Carried over thirty-four years,—O, what do you say!
Marvelous! Marvelous! and others have said the same,
There's too many wonderful things in it, even to name
And now get a book and read it, where all is made plain;
You'll think of the author over and over again.
He has eighteen grandchildren, his children number seven,
But Silas is naught, but we shall meet him in heaven,
Vesta, Silas, Ada, and Mertie, and herewith
Herbert, a lawyer, Velma, and Theodore, a blacksmith.
Martha had three children, Staples by name.
Waldin, Jennie, Nancy, remembered the same.
Nancy had five children—four boys, one girl, her pride.
Jessie, Melvin, and Harry who was shot and instantly died,
While trying to capture a burglar—doing what was right.
He'd only been married a few months when came the night.
How sudden for one so young; his prospects so fair!
We know not the day we may be called over there.
Retta and Emerson, he who to college does go,
May he stand firm for righteousness as well as to know!
Some may censure me for what I have left out;
You will like what I have written I haven't a doubt.
Good-by; may we meet where no unkind word will be spoken,
Where all will be satisfied and no *tie* broken.

www.ingramcontent.com/pod-product-compliance
Lightning Source LLC
Chambersburg PA
CBHW021941160426
43195CB00011B/1182